Thomas Cushing

Memorials of the Class of 1834 of Harvard College

Prepared for the Fiftieth Anniversary of their Graduation

Thomas Cushing

Memorials of the Class of 1834 of Harvard College
Prepared for the Fiftieth Anniversary of their Graduation

ISBN/EAN: 9783337178925

Printed in Europe, USA, Canada, Australia, Japan

Cover: Foto ©ninafisch / pixelio.de

More available books at **www.hansebooks.com**

MEMORIALS

OF

THE CLASS OF 1834

OF HARVARD COLLEGE.

PREPARED FOR THE

Fiftieth Anniversary of their Graduation,

BY

THOMAS CUSHING,

AT THE REQUEST OF HIS CLASSMATES.

BOSTON:
DAVID CLAPP & SON.
1884.

PREFACE.

By the unanimous request of the members of the HARVARD CLASS of 1834, present at the Annual Meeting, Commencement, 1883, I consented to try to bring together such simple memoirs of the dead and living as would satisfy, in a measure, the natural desire to know something of the doings of those with whom we had the peculiar and intimate relations of classmates fifty years ago. The early and lamented death of the Class Secretary, Dr. Samuel Parkman, and the absence of any regular record, has made it difficult to give a full account of some of those who died long since; but the attempt has been made to supply the omission and gain the desirable information by extensive correspondence and searching every accessible record. For the assistance that the compiler has received from various classmates he desires here to express his grateful thanks.

THOMAS CUSHING.

TABLE OF CONTENTS.

	PAGE.
PREFACE	v
LIST OF GRADUATES OF 1834	ix
NECROLOGY OF GRADUATES OF 1834 . .	xi
MEMOIRS OF THE DECEASED	1
NOTICES OF THE SURVIVORS	43
LIST OF STUDENTS SOME TIME IN THE CLASS OF 1834, WHO DID NOT GRADUATE WITH IT . . .	103
NOTICES OF STUDENTS ABOVE MENTIONED . . .	105

GRADUATES

OF THE CLASS OF 1834.

	PAGE.
WILLIAM LeROY ANNIN,	43
KINSMAN ATKINSON,	45
*GIDEON FORRESTER BARSTOW,	25
HENRY BLANCHARD,	47
EDWARD DARLEY BOIT,	52
*EDWARD BRADSTREET,	6
*CALEB ALEXANDER BUCKINGHAM,	2
※HENRY BURROUGHS,	54
*THADDEUS CLAPP,	22
※ JAMES FREEMAN COLMAN,	56
BENJAMIN EDDY COTTING,	57
*WILLIAM SMITH CRUFT,	11
THOMAS CUSHING,	62
*ELBRIDGE GERRY CUTLER,	7
*THOMAS DONALDSON,	33
FREDERIC DWIGHT,	70
*JAMES TILGHMAN EARLE,	38
SAMUEL MORSE FELTON,	70
*SAMUEL CONANT FOSTER,	29
*EDWARD FOX,	36
*EUGENE FULLER,	19
*MILES TEEL GARDNER,	27
※ HENRY GASSETT,	74
*ZEBINA MONTAGU GLEASON,	27
※ HENRY FRANCIS HARRINGTON,	75
*GEORGE HENRY HASTINGS,	15
*AARON HAYDEN,	25
※ ISAAC HINCKLEY,	76

THE CLASS OF 1834.

	PAGE.
*Rufus Hosmer,	20
*Nathaniel Babcock Ingersoll,	1
†*Benjamin Knower,	2
*Rufus Tilden King,	39
*Drausin Balthazar Labranche,	15
*Rufus Bigelow Lawrence,	5
Charles Mason,	78
*George Moore,	8
*Lucius Parker,	29
※Charles Breck Parkman,	83
*Samuel Parkman,	16
John Witt Randall,	83
*William Putnam Richardson,	19
Samuel William Rodman,	86
Joseph Sargent,	88
*Turner Sargent,	31
*William Vincent Thacher,	3
*Charles Thacher,	3
Royall Tyler,	91
※Charles Eliot Ware,	92
Charles Newell Warren,	93
Hiram Wellington,	94
Nathaniel West,	96
*Charles Henry Wheelwright,	23
†*Robert Wickliffe,	13
Joseph Hartwell Williams,	97

† Finished the college course, but did not receive their degrees in 1834, and never applied for them subsequently.

NECROLOGY.

NATHANIEL BABCOCK INGERSOLL.
Died at Brookline, Mass. . . . . March, 1836.

BENJAMIN KNOWER.
Died at Albany, N. Y. . . . . October, 1836.

WILLIAM VINCENT THACHER.
Died at Sea on voyage from Savannah, ... July 16, 1839.

CALEB ALEXANDER BUCKINGHAM.
Died at Geneva, Ill. . . . . January, 1841.

RUFUS BIGELOW LAWRENCE.
Died at Pau, France, ... Jan. 13, 1841.

EDWARD BRADSTREET.
Died at Beverly, Mass. . . . . Dec. 13, 1844.

ELBRIDGE GERRY CUTLER.
Died at Reading, Penn. . . . . April 28, 1846.

GEORGE MOORE.
Died at Quincy, Ill. . . . . March 11, 1847.

WILLIAM SMITH CRUFT.
Died at Paris, France, ... July 16, 1847.

ROBERT WICKLIFFE.
Died at Lexington, Ky. . . . . 1849.

Drausin Balthazar Labranche.
Died at St. Charles, La. . . . . Aug. 26, 1853.

George Henry Hastings.
Died at Chattanooga, Tenn. . . . . Sept. 2, 1854.

Samuel Parkman.
Died at Boston, ... Dec. 15, 1854.

William Putnam Richardson.
Died at Kendall, Ill. . . . . March 27, 1857.

Eugene Fuller.
Lost at Sea, ... June 21, 1859.

Rufus Hosmer.
Died at Lansing, Mich. . . . . April 20, 1861.

Thaddeus Clapp.
Died at Dorchester, Mass. . . . . July 10, 1861.

Charles Henry Wheelwright.
Died at the Naval Hospital, Pilotstown, Miss. . . . . . July 30, 1862.

Gideon Forrester Barstow.
Died at Fort Independence, Boston Harbor, ... June 5, 1864.

Aaron Hayden.
Died at Eastport, Maine, ... Oct. 22, 1865.

Miles Teel Gardner.
Died at Detroit, Mich. . . . . 1867.

Zebina Montagu Gleason.
Died at Westboro', Mass. . . . . Aug. 18, 1868.

Lucius Parker.
Died . . . . 1868.

NECROLOGY.

Charles Thacher.
ed at Boston, ... March 23, 1869.

Samuel Conant Foster.
ed at New York, ... April 18, 1873.

Turner Sargent.
ed at Boston, ... Feb. 24, 1877.

Thomas Donaldson.
ed at Baltimore, Md. . . . . Oct. 4, 1877.

Edward Fox.
ed at Portland, Maine, ... Dec. 14, 1881.

James Tilghman Earle.
ed at Centreville, Md. . . . . June 26, 1883.

Rufus Tilden King.
ed at Boston, ... July 7, 1883.

ADDENDUM.

Henry Burroughs.
Died at Boston. . . . . June 8, 1884.
Died, Charles P. Parkman, June 1885.
" Henry Lassett, Dec. 31, 1886.
" , Charles E. Ware, Sept. 1887.
" , Henry F. Harrington, Sept. 19, 1887.
" James F. Colman, Dec. 6, 1887.
" Isaac Hinckley, Mar. 26, 1888.

MEMOIRS OF THE DECEASED.

MEMOIRS OF THE DECEASED.

NATHANIEL BABCOCK INGERSOLL.

NATHANIEL BABCOCK INGERSOLL, son of Nathaniel and Eliza (Babcock) Ingersoll, was born in Brookline, Mass., Dec. 15, 1813. He was fitted for college at the High School in his native town. During his collegiate course, which was highly creditable to him, he lived with his widowed mother in a modest house within walking distance of the college, where his friends in the class enjoyed a simple and sweet hospitality. His personal appearance, manners, conversation, everything about him, indicated uncommon sweetness, purity and conscientiousness. Everybody loved and respected him and hoped that, with increasing years, he would acquire a physical vigor that seemed to be the only thing necessary to make his virtues and accomplishments of lasting benefit to his friends and society. But the somewhat obscure indications of consumption rapidly increased after his graduation. He filled, while he was able, with much success the position of Assistant in the High School at Brookline, where he was born and educated, and was the first of the class to pass the veil, dying in March, 1836, at the early age of twenty-two.

CHARLES KNOWER.

CHARLES KNOWER, son of Benjamin Knower, was born at Albany, N. Y., Feb. 2, 1815.

He joined the class of 1834 at the beginning of the Sophomore year, and showed himself to be a man of scholarly habits, pure tastes, and upright life and character. He was of rather a reserved nature; but those who gained his intimacy found in him a friend well worth having. Like many others of the class he did not take his degree at the close of the Senior year, and his early death, the second in the class, prevented his ever applying for it.

Soon after leaving college he began the study of the law with his brother-in-law, Gov. Marcy, so prominent in the politics of New York at that time, and after a year continued the study with Mr. Stevens, an eminent lawyer of Albany. He applied himself very closely to his studies, and bid fair to become an ornament to his profession.

In the winter of 1835 and '36 he was appointed private secretary to Gov. Marcy, which gave him an opportunity to become acquainted with men and things. In the following summer he travelled through the western country, where it is supposed he contracted the disease, bilious fever, which terminated in his death. He bore his last illness with patience and resignation, fully supported by his firm belief in Christ and the glorious promises of his religion. Thus died in the autumn of 1836, and at the early age of twenty-one, a young man of great excellence and promise.

CALEB ALEXANDER BUCKINGHAM.

CALEB ALEXANDER BUCKINGHAM, son of Joseph T. and Melinda (Alvord) Buckingham, was born in Boston, Oct. 8, 1814.

He received his preparation for college at the Boston Latin School, under Masters Gould and Leverett, and entered college in 1830. As a student he was noted especially for his fondness for argument and his readiness with his pen. He had grown up in the atmosphere of journalism, his father being editor of that well-known and popular paper, the Boston Courier, and also of a magazine, which afforded the young student a fair field to try his powers of comment on the affairs of the day and the literary topics of the time. After graduating he studied law with Gov. Ellsworth of Connecticut, and established himself at Geneva, formerly called La Fox, Kane County, Illinois, in the autumn of 1836, and resided there till his death in January, 1841, having visited Boston once in the meantime. This early death, only seven years after graduation, and the third in his class, cut him off from showing those talents and acquisitions which would almost surely have led to distinction in the new country where he had settled.

WILLIAM VINCENT AND CHARLES THACHER.

WILLIAM VINCENT and CHARLES THACHER, twin sons of Charles and Caroline (Hutchings) Thacher, were born in Boston, April 15, 1815. They were members of the same class in the Boston Latin School, where they made an excellent preparation for college, the Latin School being then in a very efficient condition. Being rather young for college life they devoted an extra year to advanced school studies, as was the case with a number of Latin School boys entering college at this time. They naturally roomed together and prosecuted their studies with about the same success, having honorable parts together in the May Exhibition of 1833. Beyond this the interesting relation between them did not, however, specially extend. There was no striking similarity of person, disposition or character. William was cautious and hard to influence. He brought everything to the test of pure reason, and cared little for popularity or the opinion of others. Charles was frank, sympathetic and impulsive.

Their lives which had run, outwardly at least, in the same channel till the close of their college course, now diverged. William, in accordance with plans of long standing, began the study of theology in the Harvard Divinity School, and Charles that of medicine in the Medical School. This separation proved final. At the close of their studies, William preached for a time at Savannah, Ga., and died while on his passage north in enfeebled health July 16, 1839, being among the first of the class to take his departure from this life.

During his short pastorate he had made himself deeply respected and beloved. His parishioners flocked on board the vessel which, it was hoped, would bear him where his health might be restored ; but this hope proving vain, they erected a tablet in his church with the following inscription :

<blockquote>
In memory of
Rev. WILLIAM VINCENT THACHER,
Pastor of this Church.

A modest and humble Christian,
the principles and precepts of his Master
which he inculcated from the pulpit
he exemplified in his own character
and illustrated by a consistent life.
Of gentle manners and warm affections,
he won many souls to Christ
by his mild and pathetic eloquence.
Those who might have resisted a bolder appeal
yielded to his calm and quiet teaching,
acknowledging the power of sincere piety
and the charms of simple goodness.
</blockquote>

Charles sailed for Havre, Nov. 10, 1837, and studied at Paris till July, 1839. He then travelled extensively in Europe, coming home to his family upon hearing the death of his brother. He did not permanently follow the profession of medicine, but became a partner in a wholesale periodical business and eventually bought the whole of it. It proved very profitable, and finally became merged in the great corporation of the American News Co. Dr. Thacher was a member of the Cincinnati; also of the Masonic fraternity. He finally fell a victim to enlargement of the liver, bearing the wasting pain of a two years' illness with marvellous patience, and dying March 23, 1869, at the age of fifty-three, in the house where he was born in Chestnut St. His last words were, "I am ready." He was a devoted and beloved son and brother, and a true and generous friend.

RUFUS BIGELOW LAWRENCE.

RUFUS BIGELOW LAWRENCE, son of Hon. Luther (H. C. 1801) and Lucy (Bigelow) Lawrence, was born in Groton, July, 1814. He attended school first at Groton and then at Stow, Mass.

He first entered college with the class of 1833, and his name appears on the first two catalogues of that class. He then left college, and rejoined it in the class of 1834 at the commencement of the Junior year.

He had a handsome person, sweet disposition and pleasant and graceful manners. These qualities gained him many friends and made him a general favorite.

After graduation he studied law in his father's office at Lowell, and began business there. In 1839 he opened an office in Boston. Life seemed to open before him in its most brilliant and attractive colors. But, unfortunately, one important element was wanting, without which all other advantages are almost useless; his health soon failed him, and symptoms of consumption manifested themselves. He spent two or three years in travel, in the hope of overcoming these alarming indications of early death; but in vain. He died at Pau, in 1841, being the fourth of the class to put off this life and enter another.

EDWARD BRADSTREET.

EDWARD BRADSTREET, son of Dr. Nathaniel (H. C. 1795) and Mary (Crombie) Bradstreet, was born in Newburyport, Mass., Nov. 10, 1813, being a direct descendant of Gov. Simon Bradstreet. He was prepared for college at the Newburyport High School, and by Hon. George Lunt, then a resident of that town. His college life was in every way creditable to him. Having lost his father not very long before entering, he seemed oppressed by the sense of his loss, and could hardly enter with spirit into the lighter occupations of the place. After graduation he studied medicine, first with Dr. R. S. Spofford of Newburyport, and afterwards, while at the Medical School in Boston, with Dr. H. I. Bowditch of that city. After finishing his medical studies, he first practised for a time at Manchester, Mass., to fill the place of the physician of that town who was disabled by sickness, and afterwards at Beverly, Mass., where he established himself, and there married Martha Jane, only daughter of Dr. Asa Woodbury of that town.

After remaining at Beverly several years, failing health compelled him to seek some place where he would be less exposed to the east winds, and he removed to Amesbury, Mass., where he established a successful practice. His health, however, entirely failed, and he died of consumption at Beverly, Dec. 13, 1844, at the early age of thirty-one.

He was extravagantly fond of his profession, and wherever he went gained always the affection and confidence of all who knew him. Had health been granted him, he would have made a successful and eminent practitioner.

ELBRIDGE GERRY CUTLER.

ELBRIDGE GERRY CUTLER, son of Nathan (Dartmouth C. 1798) and Hannah (Moore) Cutler, was born May 14, 1812, in Farmington, Maine. By the father's side he was descended from the Puritan, James Cutler of Watertown, who came to Massachusetts in 1634 from Norfolk County, England. By the death of Gen. Lincoln in 1829, his father, at that time president of the Senate, became Governor of Maine. Elbridge was a boy of a studious and serious disposition, and while but a youth joined the Congregational Church of his native town. He was prepared for college at the Farmington Academy, working during the summer on his father's farm. It is presumed that he was poorly prepared in Greek, as the examining Professor, presumably Dr. Popkin, told his father at the time of his admission, that " he might at some time have known some Greek, but he had worked it all off in the haying season." He was a faithful and conscientious student, and lived a pure and upright life, in which could plainly be seen the workings of a deeply religious nature that looked above for guidance in all the trials and temptations of life. He seemed generally under the influence of a gentle melancholy which may have been caused by the first symptoms and premonitions of the ill-health which caused his early death. For two years after leaving college, he studied law in the office of his father, and of his brother-in-law, the Hon. Robert Gardner, late of Farmington ; but he never contemplated the practice of the profession of law.

The year following he spent at the Theological Seminary at Andover, Mass., and the two years thereafter at the Divinity School at Yale College, in the pursuit of their respective courses of study, and in due course he was ordained as an Orthodox Congregational minister. In the year 1842 he was settled over the Congregational Church and Society at Belfast, Maine. There he ministered for two and a half years, to the edification of the people and with increasing influence and widening reputation, until the spring of 1846, when he was prostrated by a lung fever. After a partial recovery, in the hope that a change of climate would be beneficial to his health, he accepted an invitation to preach to the Presbyterian Society at Reading, Penn. He had been there a few weeks only and was contemplating making it his permanent residence, when he had a relapse of his illness, and, on the 28th of April, 1846, died, tenderly cared for in the family of Judge Strong, late of the U. S. Supreme Court, whose guest he was while he preached in Reading. He was an earnest, able and scholarly preacher, and a conscientious, self-sacrificing and genial gentleman.

> "None knew him but to love him,
> None named him but to praise."

In the year 1843 he married Clara Ann, daughter of Jacob Abbott, Esq., of Farmington, and sister of Rev. Jacob Abbott, the well known author, who still survives him. He had no children.

GEORGE MOORE.

GEORGE MOORE, son of Abel and Ruth Moore, was born in Sudbury, May 4, 1811. He removed to Concord when quite young, where he lived until he entered college. His life while a student was quiet, manly and industrious, commanding the respect of all. His scholarship was good and his habits most exemplary. In addition to his class-work he usually had something in hand of a remunerative nature as a partial means of support. He wrote a magnificent hand, both clerkly and elegant, an unusual accomplishment for a student, and did a great deal of work for Jared Sparks (H. C. 1815), afterwards President of the University, but then engaged on his life of Washington. The large mass of Washington's papers in Mr. Sparks's possession required a great deal of sorting, arranging and copying, for which work Mr. Moore's careful habits and excellent handwriting were eminently adapted. Nor was he the only one who did this "work with Mr. Sparks," on this and kindred matters, affording moderate remuneration for several years to those who needed and were adapted to it.

After an honorable graduation, Mr. Moore taught a young ladies' school with much success in Plymouth, Mass., for a year, and after spending another year in the Harvard Law School, as a means of mental discipline and of gaining a knowledge of affairs, he entered the Divinity School at Cambridge, as had been his intention from the beginning. From this point let his friend, fellow-student, and brother in the ministry, Rev. John H. Heywood, for many years settled at Louisville, Kentucky, take up the story of his life.

" George Moore was graduated at the Harvard Divinity School in 1839. A faithful, conscientious student, he had commanded the esteem and won the affection of his teachers and fellow-students. He went forth to the work of the ministry with a clear, vigorous, well-furnished mind, and with strong desire and resolute purpose to render the best service in his power to God and man. During the first year after his graduation he preached with great acceptance in Templeton, Northampton and other towns in Massachusetts; but his heart turned to the West. Late in the autumn of 1840 he went to Quincy, Illinois, where on the 1st of December of that year he became pastor of the Unitarian or "Second Congregational Church." Quincy, now a flourishing city, was then a small town, but very beautiful in its situation upon the banks of the Mississippi, with a fine prairie country behind it, and very attractive in its cordial, hospitable society, made up, as it was, in great measure of earnest, intelligent men and women from New England, Kentucky and other parts of the Union.

" Mr. Moore's congregation was small in numbers, but its members were devoted to their church and always ready to coöperate heartily with their pastor in all religious and humane work.

Warmly welcoming him on his arrival, respecting him thoroughly from the outset, they soon learned to love him, and his and their mutual affection became gradually deeper and stronger to the day of his death, which occurred from consumption, March 11, 1847. His ministry, though short, was very useful and he was very happy in it. He put his heart into his work. Of calm temperament, not very demonstrative, but possessing deep feelings and strong convictions, governed by principle, not impulse, he labored persistently, effectively for his church and Sunday school, for general education, for freedom, for all the highest and best interests of the community and of humanity. Frank and outspoken, his fellow citizens never doubted where he would stand in reference to any great moral cause, and they knew that, wherever he stood, he would be firm and true.

"He loved Quincy. The picturesqueness of its position, its commanding outlook, the grandeur of the noble river, the graceful outlines of the flower-gemmed, rolling prairie constantly ministered to his fine appreciation of beauty and sublimity. He loved the people and was mightily interested in them; not only in their earnest labors, but also, his sense of the humorous being very keen, in the quaintness and eccentricity which characterized some members of a community very variously composed and of marked individuality. He loved the name which the town bore, so dear to all loyal Massachusetts hearts, and he delighted to tell visiting friends, his eye twinkling as he told, how the people not content with calling the county 'Adams' and the town 'Quincy,' must call the little park in the town 'John.'

"He was very happy in his surroundings, having his home for some years in the 'Quincy House,' a hotel admirably kept by a large-hearted family from Northborough, Mass., who made it a real home to him; and for the last two years having a home of his own, presided over by his devoted and noble sister, Miss Harriet Moore, a worthy daughter of Concord.

"Mr. Moore's life and ministry were early ended. He was but thirty-six years old when he died, and his ministry altogether covered but eight years; but life and ministry were so pure in spirit, so fine and true in character and quality, that their influence was wide and pervasive and their memory is as unfading as it is fragrant."

WILLIAM SMITH CRUFT.

WILLIAM SMITH CRUFT, son of Edward and Elizabeth Storer (Smith) Cruft, was born in Pearl Street, Boston, Feb. 17, 1815. His father was an eminent Boston merchant, and his mother of the family of President John Adams's wife. He entered the Boston Latin School in August 1825, where he had the advantage of the instruction of such teachers as B. A. Gould, F. P. Leverett and E. S. Dixwell. He was a careful and conscientious student, and having finished the full course of the school entered college in 1830, well equipped for its duties. The same qualities marked his collegiate life that he had shown at school. Careful, conscientious and painstaking, he easily attained a high rank in his class, and graduated with distinction in 1834. In entering upon a college life and in his efforts to pass through it honorably, Mr. Cruft was acting more from a strong sense of duty than from personal predilection. It was well-known to his intimates, both at school and college, that his beau ideal was the life of a man of business, of a merchant in the old-fashioned and fullest sense of the word, for which he had a strong longing and eminent natural fitness; but as his father preferred that he should have the best education that the country afforded, as a preliminary to a business life, he dutifully seconded the parental wishes by his own zealous and persevering efforts.

After his graduation in 1834 he entered the counting-house of R. G. Shaw & Co., among the most eminent merchants of the day, to qualify himself for the mercantile profession, where he remained till 1836. A mind like his grasped the principles of business almost intuitively, and he was probably as well fitted for it as if he had spent seven years of his life in the counting-room, in the usual apprenticeship of those days. At the close of this year he removed to New York, and formed a copartnership with a New York merchant, under the firm name of Newbold & Cruft, as general commission merchants—a connection which continued until his death dissolved it, having meanwhile sustained the highest character for intelligence, correctness and integrity.

In 1837 Mr. Cruft visited Europe to make his house known and establish correspondence, returning in 1838. In 1841 failing health drove him again to Europe. He recovered, and on his return in 1843 married Miss Fitch, of Norwich, Conn. In 1844 he was again compelled to seek a milder climate, and went first to Madeira and thence to the continent, returning in 1846 in improved condition. His health, however, failed again, and in 1850 he left our shores for Europe never to return, dying at Paris, July 16, 1851, aged 36 years. His remains were brought home and deposited at Mt. Auburn, August 14, 1851.

In a notice of him, his pastor, Dr. Bellows, says: "No merchant of his age had a higher or more enviable place in the commercial world. His standard as a man of business was of the very highest character, and his aim and ambition as lofty as the most scrupulous moralist could desire. If Mr. Cruft had enjoyed health while engaged in business, or lived even with such health as he had through the ordinary period of a business life, we do not doubt he would have placed himself on a moral eminence as a business man that would have made him a general mark for respect and veneration in the business community."

ROBERT WICKLIFFE.

ROBERT WICKLIFFE, son of Robert and Margaret (Howard) Wickliffe, was born at Lexington, Kentucky, Dec. 28, 1815. His father was one of the most distinguished lawyers of the state, and gave his son all the advantages of a liberal education. Robert Wickliffe displayed great intelligence and assiduity in his studies. He first entered Transylvania University, where he soon took a prominent position in his classes, especially in the classical department, to the studies of which he was much devoted. Leaving Transylvania he entered Harvard in 1832, at the beginning of the Junior year. He was then a young man of lofty stature and fine presence, with fair complexion, fine features and an eagle eye. He was regular in his habits, grave in his manners, and gained the respect of all. Though reserved in his disposition his manly and honorable character made him popular with his classmates, as one proof of which he was chosen captain of the Harvard Washington Corps, a military organization of the students then in a very flourishing condition. At the time of graduation, his very positive views of what duty and honor required of him prevented his taking the steps necessary to secure a degree, as was the case with many others of the class.

He returned to Kentucky, studied law, and was admitted to the bar in his twenty-first year. For this career he was peculiarly suited, and in it he was very successful. After about three years' practice, Mr. Wickliffe was nominated as a candidate for the Legislature by the people of his native county, in which Henry Clay resided. Cassius M. Clay was also nominated, and a very bitter and exciting canvass ensued, in which Mr. Clay was elected by a few votes. Afterwards they were again rival candidates for the next Legislature. The contest became very excited, so that Mr. Clay challenged Mr. Wickliffe, though the latter was avowedly opposed to duelling. The challenge, however, was accepted, and after three shots the affair was adjusted by friends. At the ensuing election Mr. Wickliffe was elected over Mr. Clay. Afterwards, he was nominated for Congress against the Hon. Garret Davis, but was defeated, as the influence of Henry Clay, which was irresistible in the congressional districts, was exerted against him.

In the year 1849 President Tyler offered Mr. Wickliffe the position of Minister of the United States to the Kingdom of Sardinia, which he accepted. He devoted his leisure while at that court to a minute study of the life of Macchiavelli and the history of his times, with a view to a work on the subject. This was partially completed and was left unfinished at the time of his premature death. He also commenced a treatise on Constitutional Law, founded upon the Constitution of the United States in comparison with European governments.

Mr. Wickliffe returned to America at the commencement of the administration of Gen. Taylor. He had become a very accomplished French and Italian scholar, and was particularly well versed in Greek literature. He recommenced the practice of the law in Lexington with brilliant success. His early manhood was auspicious of a distinguished career; but he fell into ill-health, and died in his father's house in Lexington, in 1849, in the thirty-fourth year of his age, leaving no children.

"No man of his day in the State of Kentucky gave greater promise of legal distinction and forensic renown than Robert Wickliffe. The cast of his mind was composed, severe, and noble. He made few attempts to please, and his popularity was founded upon clearly defined principles resolutely maintained, and not upon the plausible arts usual among political leaders. His purposes were clear, and his courage immovable. His power over the Democracy preceded that of Breckenridge, and fashioned the ideas which Breckenridge afterwards advocated in Kentucky until the commencement of the war."

DRAUSIN BALTHAZAR LABRANCHE.

DRAUSIN BALTHAZAR LABRANCHE was born in St. Charles Parish, La., April 12, 1815. He came to Massachusetts in July, 1827, and prepared for college at the school of William Mills (H. C. 1796) in Cambridge.

His college life was creditable to him, while his frank and manly character and pleasant manners made him a favorite among his classmates. After graduation he studied law, and spent the rest of his life in his native town, St. Charles, dying Aug. 25, 1853.

GEORGE HENRY HASTINGS.

GEORGE HENRY HASTINGS, oldest son of Joseph Stacy Hastings, was born in Boston, June 17, 1814. He entered college from the famous Round-Hill School at Northampton. His earlier college years were not marked by the seriousness and self-consecration that characterized the later ones. Some of us cannot call to mind without a hearty laugh the escapades in which his mirthful nature and lively temperament led him to indulge. Having resided for a time at Andover, he came under influences that worked an entire change in his nature,—a case of genuine conversion or consecration of all his faculties and activities to the highest earthly objects. He says of himself in the class-book that he graduated "with the intention of becoming a missionary." Had his health been equal to his zeal and devotion, he might have become a second Brainerd or Judson. Symptoms of pulmonary consumption soon showed themselves; but he was able for several years to fill the place of chaplain to the American Legation at Rome. Finally he was obliged to leave the place on account of the rapid progress of his disease, and died at Chattanooga, Tenn., Sept. 2, 1854. During his residence at Rome, as well as during his residence and travels in the southern states, he was a regular correspondent of the New York Commercial Advertiser.

SAMUEL PARKMAN.

SAMUEL PARKMAN, son of Samuel (H. C. 1810) and Mary Bromfield (Mason) Parkman, was born in Boston, Jan. 21, 1816. He went through the full preparatory course at the Boston Latin School, and also remained for a supplementary year on account of his youth. He did not join the class in college till 1831, having pursued the studies of the Freshman year with D. G. Ingraham (H. C. 1809), an eminent instructor of that time. Being thus well prepared for college and possessed of talents, ambition and application, he took and maintained a fair rank throughout his course. He possessed the elements of popularity, having a frank and pleasant address and manners, and a fine, manly person.

At the close of the Senior year he was chosen class secretary, which office was no sinecure, owing to the stirring succession of unusual events which marked the close of the career of the class of 1834, but which it is unnecessary to recall more particularly to any member of it. The class-book shows how carefully and diligently he recorded all that seemed worthy of record of those exciting times.

No young man started in the race of life with more of the elements of success. He had a wide family connection, of great influence in financial, social and professional circles, zeal, good health and a solid substratum of good sense and good principle.

He commenced the study of medicine, and in addition to the usual three years' course, during one of which he was house-surgeon at the Massachusetts General Hospital, spent a year in study in Europe, and took his degree of M.D. in 1838. Immediately on his return, he commenced the practice of medicine and surgery in Boston, giving his attention more particularly to surgery. In 1842, in connection with his classmate, Dr. Charles E. Ware, he edited the New England Quarterly Journal of Medicine and Surgery. In the winter of 1844 he received an invitation to deliver the course of lectures upon surgery and anatomy in the Medical College at Castleton, Vermont, as successor to Dr. McClintock. This he accepted; and he repeated the course the following year; when, finding that the long absence required interfered with his professional prospects at home, he relinquished the post. In 1846, when the Massachusetts General Hospital was enlarged, he was appointed one of the new surgeons, and he continued one of its most reliable and faithful officers to the close of his life.

He was an active member of all the medical associations in the city for the advancement of science, and contributed many valuable papers. His position as a surgeon having frequently called him into court as a witness or an expert, during the last few years of his life he gave much attention to the relations of the profession to the law, and wrote two excellent articles upon it; one of which, "A Report of a Committee of the Massachusetts Medical Society upon suits for Malpractice," was read at the annual meeting of the Society in 1853,—remarkable for its clearness, candor and practical wisdom. The year before he died he was elected a Fellow of the American Academy of Arts and Sciences, and also Recording Secretary of the Massachusetts Medical Society.

One of his associates in the Society who knew him well, says of him in the pages of a medical journal:

"Of the many prominent men who have been taken from the Society by death during the past year (1854), although one of the youngest, no one has left a wider vacancy than Dr. Samuel Parkman. Always active and interested in the general welfare of his profession and in everything that related to it, he felt a

special interest in that spirit of progress which requires the
energy and ambition of youth for its advancement. His fine
person and manly bearing were but the result and expression of
his eminently manly character. Accomplished in the science of
his profession; candid and cautious in his judgment, and most
conscientiously faithful to his duty; kind, disinterested and
humane, he was a man to be relied upon for his opinions, and
to be trusted in action. In his social relations he was a faithful,
warm, and honest friend; at hand in the hour of trial; sympa-
thizing in the hour of joy, and true and frank when a friendly
and, it might be, an unpleasant truth was to be told. An almost
morbid hostility to anything like pretension, so as to make him
uncharitable, perhaps, to so common and venial a weakness,
was a most marked feature in his character. He always appeared
less than he was himself, because he feared to claim that which
he was not. At the hour when he was beginning to become
more widely known, when he was beginning to exercise the influence which sterling merit and well-tried character must always
exercise, the mysterious hand of Providence has struck him down,
and the profession is called upon to mourn one of its ablest and
best friends."

Dr. Parkman married Mary Eliot, daughter of Edmund
Dwight, Esq., and left two children, a son and daughter, the
former of whom, Mr. Henry Parkman, a young lawyer, has already made his mark as an able and upright member of our
municipal government, and active participator in our state politics, exhibiting the same uprightness, straight-fordwardness and
sterling honesty of character which distinguished his father.

WILLIAM PUTNAM RICHARDSON.

WILLIAM PUTNAM RICHARDSON, son of William P. and Deborah (Lang) Richardson, was born at Salem, Mass., Aug. 15, 1813. He received his entire preliminary training in the Grammar and Latin School of his native town, and, entering in 1830, passed quietly and respectably through college. His habits were careful and exact, and his attention to his duties regular and conscientious. After graduation he immediately began the study of medicine in the office of Dr. A. L. Peirson (H. C. 1812) of Salem, and received the degree of M.D. from the Harvard Medical School in 1837. He entered upon practice at Salem, where he continued until 1846, when he removed to Kendall, Kendall County, Illinois. Here he was chiefly engaged in agricultural and horticultural pursuits, for which his careful habits, fine taste, and love of natural history particularly fitted him. He died at Kendall, March 27, 1857. Dr. Richardson was never married.

EUGENE FULLER.

EUGENE FULLER, oldest son of Hon. Timothy (H. C. 1801) and Margaret (Crane) Fuller, was born in Cambridge, Mass., May 14, 1815. His father was a prominent figure in the political, as his sister Margaret was in the literary life of their times. Eugene received his early education in the schools of Cambridge. "At the end of the first term of the Sophomore year," as he says in the Class Book, becoming tired of college, "I became convinced that nature intended me for a merchant. Accordingly I went into a counting-room in Boston, but at the end of a week became convinced that nature intended me for no such thing; returned gladly to college at the beginning of the Junior year, and remained there contentedly till the present era" (Graduation). After leaving college Mr. Fuller studied law, partly in the law school at Cambridge and partly in the office of George F. Farley, Esq. (H. C. 1816), of Canton, Mass. After his admission to the bar he practised his profession two years at Charlestown, Mass. He afterwards went to New Orleans, and was connected with the public press of that city. He spent several summers there, and two or three years before his death was affected by a sunstroke, resulting in a softening of the brain, which came very near proving fatal, and left him in a shattered condition. His friends hoping that medical treatment at the North might benefit him, he embarked with an attendant on board the Empire City for New York. When one day out, his attendant being prostrated with sea-sickness, Mr. Fuller was left alone and was not afterwards seen. He must have been lost overboard June 21, 1859. The New Orleans Picayune, with which paper he was for sometime connected, in its issue of June 30th, says of Mr. Fuller: "His industry, reliability and intelligence were equalled only by his invariably mild, correct, and gentlemanly demeanor, and he was liked and respected by all who knew him." Mr. Fuller married Mrs. Rotter, a widow lady of New Orleans, originally of Philadelphia. They had five children, three sons and two daughters.

RUFUS HOSMER.

RUFUS HOSMER, son of Hon. Rufus (H. C. 1800) and Amelia (Paine) Hosmer, was born in Stow, Mass., July 16, 1816. By both the paternal and maternal side he was sprung from the best colonial and revolutionary stock. He was fitted for college at the academy in Stow. His college life was quiet and uneventful, and he received his degree in 1834.

After leaving college he studied law in his father's office at Stow, and attended lectures at the Law School at Cambridge. In 1838 he went to Michigan, and soon afterwards was admitted to the bar. He began the practice of his profession at Pontiac, Michigan, at first in partnership with his cousin, Charles Draper (H. C. 1833), and afterwards with the late George Wisner. He was very successful, and attained a high rank as a lawyer; but after a few years he relinquished the profession, removed to Detroit, and became editor of the Daily Advertiser in that city. He held this position about seven years, when, having been appointed state printer, it became necessary for him to reside in the capital of the state. He accordingly removed to Lansing, where he became part owner and editor of the Lansing Advertiser. Here he remained about three years, and relinquished his situation a few days before his death to accept the appointment of consul at Frankfort-on-the-Main. While making preparations for his departure to his foreign post, he was prostrated by an attack of apoplexy, which terminated his life after a few days' illness. As an editor, and an agreeable and finished writer, he had few superiors; but it was for his eminent social qualities, his keen wit, his ready repartee, and his powers of conversation that he was best known and most admired in the various communities in which he resided.

He married in 1840 Sarah Chamberlin, daughter of Dr. Olmsted Chamberlin of Pontiac, his wife surviving him, as did also two daughters and a son.

THADDEUS CLAPP.

THADDEUS CLAPP, the second son and third child of Capt. William and Elizabeth (Humphreys) Clapp, was born in Dorchester, Mass., May 11, 1811. He was fitted for college at the Academy of Hiram Manley (H. C. 1825) in Dorchester. In college he was a grave, dignified and conscientious student, always gentle and mild in speech and manners, and faithful in every respect. No one profited more, if so much, by the excellent instruction of Dr. Beck in the Latin language, some of whose methods, then novel in America, had excited much interest and zeal in that study, through which and his own application Mr. Clapp became one of the best Latin scholars of his time. He attained a high general rank, and graduated very high in the class. Immediately after leaving college he taught a private school in Brookline for a short time. He was superintendent of the Sunday School of the First Church and Society in Dorchester for about two years from 1836. On the 16th of February, 1837, he entered his name with Col. Loammi Baldwin of Charlestown, as a student of Engineering; but on account of ill-health he did not prosecute his studies. On taking his degree of A.M. in 1837, the Latin Valedictory Oration was offered him by President Quincy, which, on account of feeble health, he could not accept. He was secretary of the Board of School Committee in Dorchester several years, and wrote some of the annual reports; among them those for the years 1842 and 1843, which were printed. In the fall of 1838 he went to Franklin, La., where he was for six or seven months a tutor in the family of Wm. L. Palfrey, Esq., brother of Rev. J. L. Palfrey (H. C. 1815). He returned to Dorchester in 1839. No doubt this visit to the south strengthened the anti-slavery convictions which his conscientiousness and love of justice had led him already to feel. About the year 1840 he engaged in horticultural and pomological pursuits, which he continued to follow during his life. He became quite celebrated among fruit growers for his theoretical and practical knowledge, and obtained many premiums for fine samples of choice varieties of fruit, and became a member of the Mass. Horticultural and Norfolk Agricultural Societies. He was of a most amiable disposition, and led a life of the most conscientious and unspotted integrity. Feeble health alone prevented his occupying more conspicuous positions in the world's estimation. He died July 10, 1861. He married in Claremont, N. H., August, 1857, Mary H. Dustin, daughter of Rev. Caleb Dustin, and a descendant of Hannah Dustin, so celebrated in the early history of New Hampshire, who survives him.

CHARLES HENRY WHEELWRIGHT.

CHARLES HENRY WHEELWRIGHT, son of Lot and Susannah (Wilson) Wheelwright, was born in Purchase Street, Boston, May 29, 1814. At the age of ten years he spent a year at the Round-Hill School at Northampton, and some time subsequently at Mr. Greene's Academy at Jamaica Plain. His health being delicate, he completed his preparation as a pupil of Hon. Jonathan Chapman (H. C. 1825), travelling at intervals to improve his bodily condition, and entering the Sophomore class in 1831. He subsequently was obliged to obtain a year's leave of absence for the same reason, spending it mostly at the South. His genial disposition and frank and pleasant manners made him a general favorite among those who knew him. In his Senior year he was adjutant of the Harvard Washington Corps, the military organization of the day. For the same reasons that influenced others of his classmates he did not take his degree at the close of his Senior year, and, being absent from the country most of his subsequent life, never applied for it; but at the request of his classmates, it was conferred upon him in 1875, thirteen years after his death. He studied medicine in the office of Dr. Geo. C. Shattuck, of Boston, and received the degree of M.D. in 1837.

Having decided to enter the navy, he offered himself for examination at Philadelphia, passed the third on the list, and was commissioned assistant surgeon in 1839. He was appointed to the sloop of war Marion in 1843; to the receiving ship Ohio and frigate Independence of the home squadron in 1845. He was next appointed to the Naval Hospital at Pensacola, a very unhealthy position, of great labor and responsibility. After very arduous services during the prevalence of malarial fever, he was taken ill of it himself, came very near dying, and was never in firm health afterwards. He joined the Mediterranean squadron in 1848, and in 1850 was ordered to California by way of the Isthmus. In 1852 he went with the Powhatan on the Japanese expedition, and was promoted to a full surgeoncy on the Plymouth in 1860 and 1861. He did duty at the Brooklyn navy yard, and on the Board of Examining Surgeons, a place at that time of great labor and responsibility.

Not aware of his own feebleness he applied for more active service, and was appointed to the San Jacinto, March 9th, and ordered to Hampton Roads to take part in the expected sea-fight, after which his friends never saw him again. He missed orders to go North in the Colorado by forty-eight hours. Had he received them he would have been saved from another summer in the Gulf, which in his feeble health he dreaded.

Orders came to him to take charge of the Naval Hospital at Pilotstown, at the S. W. pass of the Mississippi, a most arduous position, where without proper appliances or necessary assistance he had to struggle with sickness and death in the most appalling forms. Worn down by incessant work, he wrote in a prophetic spirit, but with unabated courage: "I have been here a week, have only one assistant, and am weak from want of sleep and diarrhœa. There is no way to get relief from my situation. I shall do my duty to the end."

He died July 30, 1862, a true martyr to his duty and his country, of whom as their only representative in the active service of the war of the rebellion his classmates may be proud.

GIDEON FORRESTER BARSTOW.

GIDEON FORRESTER BARSTOW, son of Dr. Gideon and Nancy (Forrester) Barstow, was born in Salem, Dec. 23, 1815.

He received his preparatory education at the Salem Latin School, and joined the class at the beginning of the Sophomore year in 1831. Immediately upon graduation he commenced the study of medicine, which he practised first in New York and subsequently in Salem. Relinquishing this profession he became a civil engineer, working upon railroads in northern Massachusetts and Connecticut. Marrying Miss Mary Cogswell, a physician's daughter in Connecticut, he resumed the practice of medicine in that state. During the war of the rebellion surgeon-general Dale, of Massachusetts, appointed him to a post in Fort Warren, Boston Harbor, where he died suddenly June 5, 1864, leaving a widow and one son.

AARON HAYDEN.

AARON HAYDEN, son of Aaron and Ruth (Jones) Hayden, was born at Eastport, Maine, Sept. 23, 1814.

He attended school at Washington Academy, East Machias, Me., and finished his preparation for college at South Reading Academy. His college life was quiet and uneventful. He attended strictly to the objects for which he came to college, and had the respect of all who knew him.

After graduating in 1834, he pursued his studies for three years at the Cambridge Law School. He was admitted to the bar in 1838, and commenced the practice of law in his native town of Eastport, to which he was fondly attached, and where he contentedly spent his life, though his talents and acquisitions would have adorned a wider sphere. In each of the years, 1844 and 1845, he was elected to the House of Representatives of his native state, and, in 1856, he was a member of the State Senate. In these public positions he distinguished himself as a dignified and wisely practical legislator, and an effective debater. His political sentiments were moderate, conservative and national. When, at a later period of his life, the existence of the national government was imperilled, he ardently embraced the cause of the constitution and the Union, and zealously labored with his voice and pen for their maintenance and preservation.

Mr. Hayden was interested from early years in religious subjects, and the extent and variety of his theological inquiries were remarkable. Though educated in the religious tenets of his family, he took nothing upon trust, but with conscientious independence following his own investigations to their natural results, on the 30th of November, 1864, he received confirmation as a member of the Episcopal church.

Months before his departure, struck down by a sudden and well nigh instantaneously fatal stroke of apoplexy, he rallied but partially from the attack. Loving life, yet not fearing death, he resisted its progress with heroic firmness, and performed his duties with entire steadiness, until at last, forced to yield to its irresistible power, he calmly, peacefully and hopefully met his fate on the 22d of October, 1866.

Mr. Hayden married Miss Jane Briggs, of Robbinston, Me., June 10, 1847, and left one son, Aaron Hayden, Esq., now also of Robbinston.

MILES TEEL GARDNER.

MILES TEEL GARDNER, son of Miles and Lydia (Teel) Gardner, was born at West Cambridge, Mass., Jan. 31, 1808.

After graduation he became a teacher, and taught with much success at various places, among them Arlington and Dedham, Mass. He then became interested in business as a dealer in school books at Rochester, N. Y., and, subsequently, in seeds and agricultural implements at Detroit, Michigan.

He was succeeding fairly in this business when he was attacked by consumption, and died in 1867.

Honesty of purpose and fidelity in action were his special characteristics, and he always commanded the esteem and respect of those among whom he lived.

ZEBINA MONTAGU GLEASON.

ZEBINA MONTAGU GLEASON, son of Elijah and Lucy (Fay) Gleason, was born in Westborough, Mass., Dec. 10, 1810.

His health, always delicate, rendered him unable to work upon his father's farm, as most farmers' sons at that time were expected to do, and he early showed a love for reading and study. After attending the district and select schools in his native town, he was sent to Amherst Academy, and thence to Leicester, where he was prepared for Harvard.

After graduating he began the study of law with Samuel B. Walcott (H. C. 1819), of Hopkinton, Mass. Fletcher Webster (H. C. 1833) was his fellow student. In 1836 he went to Troy,

N. Y., where he continued his legal studies with George N. Titus, Esq. of that city, and the following year was admitted to the New York bar. While in Troy he was much interested in politics, wrote many articles for the press, and engaged in frequent and animated discussions on the political questions of the day. In 1838 he was licensed to practise as Attorney at Law, in the courts of Illinois, having been admitted to the bar in that state. The following year he returned to Westborough, and was married to Miss Mary L. Harrington of that town, May, 1839. She died Oct. 7, 1841, leaving no children. Subsequently Mr. Gleason taught a select school for many years in his native town, and on June 10th, 1847, was again married to Miss Caroline B. Clarke, of Framingham.

By the death of his father in 1850, he became almost by necessity, as well as by inclination, a farmer, and was an enterprising, intelligent, and progressive leader in agricultural pursuits. Although residing in the village, he took great pride and pleasure in owning and successfully cultivating the "homestead farm," which had been in possession of his family for four generations. His interest in the schools of the town was lifelong, and during his official connection with them he endeavored to raise their standard and awaken in every scholar a desire to attain a degree of excellence that would fit him for useful activity in life.

Mr. Gleason died of carditis Aug. 18, 1868. He left six children, of whom two graduated at Harvard University in the class of '71 and '78, respectively. One who knew him well says : "Mr. Gleason possessed strong traits of character, of which genuineness was a leading one. He despised all shams, and, although naturally very reserved, had great self-reliance. He arrived at his conclusions after long and patient thought, and, once formed, he required proof positive to change his opinion. His domestic attachments were peculiarly strong, and he ever showed himself a kind and affectionate husband and father."

LUCIUS PARKER.

LUCIUS PARKER, son of Rev. Jeroboam Parker (H. C. 1797), was born in Southborough, Mass., Sept. 3, 1807.

Mr. Parker first entered college with the class of 1833, but leaving sometime during the Freshman year, reëntered with that of 1834. Being a mature man at the time of entrance and strongly under the influence of religious principle and feeling, his college life was marked by dignity, gravity and strict attention to study. Such men are an advantage to any college class, as they in some measure balance the immaturity and light-headedness of the majority, and do good by quiet example. As an expression of this feeling of respect and confidence it is recorded in the Class-Book, March 11, 1834, that Mr. Parker was chosen Chaplain for the Class Day exercises, and on Class Day it is recorded that "the meeting was opened by prayer from the Chaplain, Mr. Parker."

Entering the ministry after graduation, Mr. Parker identified himself with the Methodist persuasion, in which he rose to be a Bishop, officiating in Wisconsin and other north-western states.

He was twice married, and died in 1868, having been a faithful and lifelong worker in the Christian vineyard.

SAMUEL CONANT FOSTER.

SAMUEL CONANT FOSTER, son of Dr. Andrew (H. C. 1800) and Mary (Conant) Foster, was born Oct. 24, 1817, at Jamaica Plain, Mass.

He made his preparation for college at the well-known school of Charles W. Greene (H. C. 1802) at Jamaica Plain, and entered at the early age of thirteen, being less than a year younger than Warren, the most youthful member of the class. On his graduation in 1834, he commenced the study of medicine in the office of Dr. Winslow Lewis, of Boston, and received the degree of M.D. at the Jefferson Medical College, Philadelphia, in 1837, when he was but twenty years old. He then went abroad, studied in London and Paris, and spent six months in the Dublin Lying-in Hospital. After nearly three years' absence, he returned home and began practice in New York in 1839. He became, in a short time, one of the Physicians to the New York Dispensary, and in 1852 was appoined one of the Visiting Physicians to Bellevue Hospital, which post he held for nearly six years, doing faithful duty and being always respected for his skill. He held numerous places of honor in the profession. He was Vice President of the Academy of Medicine, Secretary and afterwards Vice President of the New York Society for the Relief of the Widows and Orphans of Medical Men, and was an active member of several other learned societies.

In 1857 he married Mary B., daughter of Mr. Theodore P. Bogert, of New York, by whom he had five children, four of whom survived him.

In 1859 severe attacks of pleuritis and sciatica forced him to give up business almost entirely for three or four years; and when partial recovery enabled him to resume practice, he gradually reëstablished himself; but just as he had obtained an enviable place in his profession, tuberculosis manifested itself and he was obliged to break off again.

The rest of his life was a pursuit after health, with brief intervals of professional practice. He visited Colorado, made a voyage in a sailing vessel, visiting Cadiz, Marseilles and Paris, and finally, as a last resort, removed his family to Nassau, New Providence. Here he was able to cheer the sick and do something to relieve the sufferings of many who were, like himself, seeking health in a foreign land. He calmly watched the progress of his disease, and died most peacefully on the 18th of April, 1873, in the full possession of his faculties, and conscious to the last.

The memorial from which the above facts are mostly taken says of him : " Dr. Foster was a man of clear and vigorous intellect, nurtured in the best schools of literature and medicine, and ripened by large experience in hospital and private practice. He was a rare scholar, calm, judicious, logical, and just.

" His family relations were of the most tender and loving. He was a good citizen, eminently patriotic, and his dealings with all men were marked by the strictest integrity.

" His contributions to medical literature were not many, but of superior excellence. Everything that came from his pen showed care and elegance. Critical over his own writings, he was prompt to detect the least departure from good taste in others.

" As a medical practitioner he was calmly thoughtful, taking great pains in the investigation of his cases, attentive to his patients, and doing his duty conscientiously.

" His opinions were valued by the profession, and he brought forward to enforce them a full storehouse of knowledge, gathered from careful study and from his own private experience."

Among his writings on medical subjects may be mentioned his essay on " Atelectasis of the Lungs in Young Infants," and his paper on " Mammary Abscesses." Besides these is his paper " On Phenomena observed in a case of Epilepsy," and his most finished production, his Oration before the New York Academy of Medicine.

TURNER SARGENT.

TURNER SARGENT, son of Henry and Hannah (Welles) Sargent, was born in Dorchester, Mass., August 11, 1813.

His preparation for college was made chiefly at the Boston Latin School, being interrupted from time to time by the delicacy of his health, an obstacle with which he had to contend through life. He entered at the beginning of the second term of the Sophomore year, early in January, 1832. Like others of the class he did not take his degree at the close of the course, but received it in 1835. Much of Mr. Sargent's life was spent in travelling and in foreign countries; but though he gained somewhat in vigor towards middle life, he never undertook continuous or professional labor. Having a refined taste and sympathetic and generous heart, he was able to benefit the community in many ways in his position as a private gentleman of means and leisure, by the exercise of those qualities. Such men are highly useful in a community where the high pressure activity of business life does not spare many men for the important services tending to refine, improve, and elevate. In this connection it seems fitting to introduce a letter growing out of a conversation with a mutual friend, the pastor of the First Church in Boston, where Mr. Sargent had long attended.

106 Marlborough Street,
March 22, 1884.

Dear Mr. Cushing:

You asked me about your classmate and my parishioner, Mr. Turner Sargent, who is no more with us. I was glad to be so inquired of. For as the minister of the First Church, and in my personal relations to that gentleman, I owe him a debt which it is pleasant to acknowledge. He was a member of the Standing Committee of that Church when I was installed as its pastor, and, save with such interruptions as were necessary on account of his frequent absences from the country, or were caused by the severe illnesses of his last years, he was diligent in the discharge of the duties of that trust, and singularly and most usefully so during the very trying transition and transplanting of the congregation from Chauncy to Marlborough St. He was of the utmost service in planning and building the new house of worship, and in guiding to satisfactory issues the changes in the forms of service, which were then proposed and carried into effect. Mr. Sargent was a man of deep, tender, and genuine religious sensibilities, and eager to recover much which is precious in this way, but had been inevitably dropped for the time by an over anxious Puritanism. He well understood that our so-called congregational worship is extremely objective and too much dependent on the moods of the officiating minister, and not sufficiently expressive of Christian consciousness in acts of common prayer. He was a churchly man, in the best sense of that word, very broad and receptive of new forms of truth;

but also careful of the old Christian treasure, and more engaged to fulfil than to destroy. We of the First Church owe much to his generosity —his gifts of time, money, counsel, honorable methods in the business affairs of the Church, the spirit of a high-toned man of affairs applied (as it so often fails to be) to Christian institutions. Quietly, in his own way, he came into the open communion of the congregation. He loved the house of God as the place concerning which He had said, "My name shall be there." He always helped me all that he honestly could. He was patient, considerate, charitable in his judgments, and whilst he cherished his own religious convictions he had a kind side for much which he could accept only in part. The Church will always point with delight and pride to the Sargent window memorial of his father in his eyes, but in our eyes of him as well, and a witness to his appreciation of the mystic element in our Divine Faith. I shall be glad in any record which you have to make of him to be numbered with the remnant of elders still lingering in First Church among Mr. Sargent's warm friends.

Yours in pleasant remembrance of past years,

RUFUS ELLIS.

Mr. Sargent was twice married, but left no children. His health gradually declined, and he died Feb. 24, 1877.

THOMAS DONALDSON.

THOMAS DONALDSON, the oldest son of John Johnston and Caroline (Dorsey) Donaldson, was born in Baltimore, May 8th, 1815. His ancestors on both sides were of Irish extraction, and had been conspicuous and patriotic citizens of their adopted country.

At about the age of ten years he was sent to Round-Hill School, at Northampton, where he remained for five years, entering the Freshman class at Harvard in April, 1831. Here his fine natural abilities and good preliminary training enabled him to take high rank as a scholar, while his sweet disposition and gentle and conciliatory manners made him a general favorite among his classmates and acquaintances. It is hardly necessary to recall to any member of the class of 1834 the circumstances under which we parted at the close of our Senior year, involving the suspension of their degrees to several of high standing both as students and gentlemen. These were subsequently given to all who applied for them. Mr. Donaldson never applied for his;* but in 1851 it was voluntarily conferred on him by the college, which, like an honorary degree, may be considered a tribute to his character and position. This is mentioned as it may not be generally known, and shows the softening influence of time in the views of governing bodies.

After leaving Harvard, he began the study of the law in Baltimore; but his health failing, he began the active duties of life as a civil engineer, and was employed in the construction of various railroads. During this period, in the year 1838, he married his cousin, Elizabeth Pickering Dorsey, of Boston, granddaughter of Col. Timothy Pickering, of Massachusetts. Eleven children were born of this marriage, nine of whom and their mother and seven grandchildren survived him.

When his health was sufficiently reëstablished, he commenced the more congenial study of the law, and came to the bar in 1843. About this time he purchased some acres of land in a high and picturesque tract called Elkridge, eight miles from Baltimore. In this place, which he called Edgewood, he built a comfortable house, which it was his pleasure to adorn with all that endears a home, and where he resided the rest of his life.

In the years 1847 and 1848 he served as a member of the House of Delegates of Maryland, filling the difficult and important position of Chairman of the Committee of Ways and Means. Maryland had become a defaulting State, and for some years had ceased to pay interest on her debt. This state of things was intolerable to the upright and honorable mind of Mr. Donaldson, and he devoted himself to the removal of this stain upon the honor of his native State. He was unwearied in his

---

* As stated in a Memorial Sketch of him published in Baltimore in 1851.

efforts to effect the prompt restoration of the public credit, and had the satisfaction in 1847 to see Maryland place herself, through her legislature, on the list of solvent States, to which result no one had contributed more than himself. Mr. Donaldson also took an active and useful part in the Constitutional Convention called in 1850 to make a new constitution for the State of Maryland.

When the war of secession broke out, the position of the citizens of Maryland was difficult in the extreme; but Mr. Donaldson was always a steady and conscientious upholder of the cause of the Union, though he never allowed his patriotic feelings to alienate his personal friendships. In Howard County where he resided, and where he was the recognized leader of the bar, he was surrounded by loving and anxious friends and neighbors.

In the winter of 1876-7 his health began seriously to fail, the malady proving to be Bright's disease. He was advised to try the effect of a warmer and drier climate, and accordingly he went in the following spring, accompanied by his wife, to Aiken, S. C., and afterwards to Charleston. The change brought temporary relief, but he returned home not essentially benefited. Understanding his own condition, he set to work diligently to put his affairs in order, especially those in which he was concerned as trustee; but he was not able to resume his professional practice. On the 20th of July, 1877, he was struck by paralysis, and died on the 4th of October.

The tribute paid to the deceased by the Hon. Chief Justice Brown, of Baltimore, will convey an accurate estimate of his professional standing:

" Profoundly read in law, he added to knowledge soundness of judgment and great skill in the trial of causes. His ready and retentive memory carried all the points and facts of a long and intricate case from the beginning to the close. His mind was both minute and comprehensive. His presentation of the law in the papers which he drew was singularly clear, exact and exhaustive. His examination and cross-examination of witnesses were conducted with marked ability, and, when the testimony was closed, his side of the cause was presented to the jury with persuasive and forcible eloquence, making him always a formidable opponent.

"Nor did he at any time neglect, during a life of unusual toil and many cares, the broader culture which none need so much as men of engrossing professional pursuits. He was a ripe and graceful scholar, and illustrated in his fine and graceful elocution his thorough familiarity with the best literature of the English tongue. It is no wonder, therefore, that the public respect for his abilities and the universal confidence reposed in him were warmed by feelings of admiration and affection. Among his professional brethren his popularity was unqualified. In private and social life no one could be more universally esteemed, for no one could be more faithful than he to all its duties and in all its relations, more true as a friend or more delightful as a companion. Those who knew him best were those who loved him most, for only they could know with what sufferings and trials it was his fate to struggle, or with how much of manly and Christian fortitude and courage he rose above them all."

EDWARD FOX.

EDWARD FOX, son of John and Lucy Jones (Oxnard) Fox, was born in Portland, Me., June 10, 1815. He received his early training in the public schools of his native city. After graduating from the High School he was sent to Phillips Academy, Exeter, N. H., where he finished his preparation for college, and entered in 1830. He was a successful student, graduating with honor in 1834. Entering as a boy, he grew literally in every direction, recording of himself in the class book, that he increased in height *fifteen* inches during his college course. He immediately entered the Harvard Law School, where he spent three years, and received the degree of LL.B. He was admitted to the Cumberland County bar, and began practice with R. A. L. Codman, Esq., under the firm name of Codman & Fox, which partnership lasted till 1848 or 1849. He married a daughter of Nathan Winslow, of Portland, for his first wife. For the benefit of her health he removed to Cincinnati, where he practised his profession part of a year. After her death he returned to Portland, and was soon after elected City Solicitor, and discharged the duties of this office with credit to himself and the profession.

While he was City Solicitor he was elected County Attorney, and in 1862 he was appointed a judge of the Supreme Court of the State of Maine. He resigned this office soon after, and entered into partnership with his brother Frederic, under the firm name of E. & F. Fox. In 1866 he was appointed to succeed Judge Ware as District Judge of the U. S. Court, which important position he held till his death.

It will thus be seen that Mr. Fox's life illustrates the successive steps of the successful lawyer, and the esteem and confidence of his fellow citizens and the general government.

His second wife, who survives him, was Mrs. Fessenden, her maiden name being Trask. His first wife left two children, a son and a daughter. The son, Edward Winslow Fox, became a member of the Cumberland bar, and gave high promise of eminence in his profession. His health was poor, and in company with his father he took a journey to the South. He died at Savannah in 1877, and his father returned with the dead body of his son. It is thought that Judge Fox never fully recovered from the shock caused by the death of his son.

Judge Fox was one of the most prominent and successful lawyers in Maine, and, while in the practice of his profession, he carried on an immense business. He successfully brought to an issue many very important cases, which will be remembered by the older members of the bar and citizens of Portland.

Though he always took a keen interest in public affairs and was fitted for any position in the gift of his fellow-citizens, the judge held himself aloof from all political discussions and party movements. He never tried to gain the good will of any party or individual except by plain straight-forward dealing. His stern integrity, uncompromising love of justice and antique simplicity, with his grand and massive presence, made him almost the ideal judge.

JAMES TILGHMAN EARLE.

JAMES TILGHMAN EARLE, son of R. T. and Mary (Tilghman) Earle, was born in Centreville, Queen Anne's County, Maryland, July 13, 1814. His father was for many years the chief judge of the Judicial District, composed of Queen Anne's, Cecil, Kent and Talbot Counties. He was for many years conspicuous in the politics of Maryland. His advent into political life was as a Democrat, in the hazardous campaign of 1864, when he was elected to the Senate of Maryland, where he remained five consecutive terms, serving nearly all that time as Chairman of the Finance Committee. During the session of 1872 he brought forward the Chesapeake and Delaware Ship Canal project.

He was also largely identified with the agricultural interests and practical education of farmers in Maryland. It was very largely through him that steps were taken for the endowment with public lands of the Maryland Agricultural College. He was also at one time president of the Maryland Agricultural Society.

He died at his residence in Centreville, July 15, 1882, of general prostration, resulting from malaria.

RUFUS TILDEN KING.

RUFUS TILDEN KING, son of Major Rogers and Mary (Tilden) King, was born in West Medford, Mass., May 21, 1807. He was prepared for college at the Academy in Stow, Mass., and entered for the first time in 1829. He remained in this class (that of 1833) for two years, holding a high rank among men so eminent for scholarship as many of its members subsequently became. He was the room-mate, for a part of the time at least, of Fletcher Webster, and through him became well acquainted with Daniel Webster, who strongly encouraged him to study the law, considering that his mind was well adapted to that profession. His health failing, he was obliged to leave college for a year, and when he returned, though strongly urged by President Quincy to rejoin his own class, he entered the next one, thus graduating in 1834. After graduating he began the study of the law in the office of Hon. Luther Lawrence of Lowell (H. C. 1801); but, his health continuing delicate, he was obliged to abandon his preparation for the bar. Soon after he went to Yarmouth, N. S., where he held the position of principal of Yarmouth Academy for some time. After the death of his first wife, Emeline E. Stone, of Framingham, in 1845, he taught for several years in the well known private school of Charles W. Greene (H. C. 1802) at Jamaica Plain. While there he married Miss Chloe W. Smith. He next went to New York, where he met with marked success in classical teaching. The latter years of his life Mr. King spent in Fernandina, Florida, where he devoted his time to the cultivation of oranges, rather as a means of improving his health than as a source of profit. He died while on a visit to Boston, July 3, 1883.

A cotemporary notice speaks of him as follows: "A man of great intellect, a close and accurate scholar, an affectionate son, husband and brother, ever making friends and never losing them, feeling a strong interest in all matters of religion and philanthropy, his death will cast a deep shadow over all with whom his long life has been so pleasantly connected."

NOTICES OF THE SURVIVORS.

NOTICES OF THE SURVIVORS.

WILLIAM LEROY ANNIN.

OUR classmate modestly introduces his Autobiography with a quotation, with some small changes, from one of his favorite classics.

> "Coactus assiduis tuis vocibus, Cushing, quam quotidiana mea recusatio non difficultatis excusationem sed inertiæ videretur deprecationem habere, difficillimam rem suscepi. Hanc vitam utinam qui legent scire possint quam invitus susceperim scribendam, quo facilius caream stultitiæ atque arrogantiæ crimine qui me mediis interposuerim Harvardi-anorum scriptis."

I was born in Le Roy, Genesee County, N. Y., July 28, 1812, the eldest of the seven children of Joseph and Melinda (Weld) Annin, my birth being coeval with the organization of my native town. After attending various public and private schools, I finished my preparation for college at the new school on Temple Hill, Geneseo, recently opened by Messrs. Cleaveland, Felton and Sweetser, recent graduates of Harvard. After spending two years here I opened a small private school in Le Roy, continuing my studies till, in the fall of 1831, I joined the Sophomore class at Harvard, and graduated in 1834. While in college I taught private pupils and also public schools in the towns of Canton and Shrewsbury, Mass. After graduation I taught, sometimes as principal and sometimes as assistant, in both public and private schools and academies, in the towns of Le Roy, N. Y., Cambridge, Mass., in Boston, at the High School at Jamaica Plain, in Mr. Charles W. Greene's School, at Watertown and Concord, Mass., and at various places in New York, for longer or shorter terms; and for many years have had private pupils at the same time.

I was also employed as surveyor on the lines of the Lexington and Old Colony Railroads, and in the distribution of the Commonwealth newspaper in anti-slavery times.

In 1852 I returned to Le Roy, my native place, where I have since resided, doing more or less private teaching, lecturing occasionally, and assisting in the management of my brother's reading-room. More recently my time has been partly occupied in horticultural and agricultural pursuits.

Never inclined to rest in scepticism, baptized in babyhood in the Presbyterian faith, and in youth confirmed in the Episcopal Church, at one time I became a member of the Congregational Church in Le Roy, which may now be said to have disbanded, since most of the members have gone to far better homes than they had here. At Harvard, however, I attended the Chapel services, where we then had those good preachers, Henry Ware, Jr. and Dr. Palfrey.

In my Junior year, in company with my classmate, Felton, I made a pedestrian tour to the White Mountains, made the ascent of Mt. Washington, stood upon the top of Red Mountain, and got quite a general idea of the scenery of three of the New England States.

Listening and reading rather than talking or writing seem to have been my characteristic; but partial deafness has now changed all that. Once I was advanced in French and German; but I was obliged partly to give up the modern languages for the classic authors. Some modern historians have drawn largely upon my time, and I am not so much troubled as formerly with historic doubts. I think, perhaps, I owe something to the forcible illustration of the "Higher Law," presented in the anti-slavery discussions before the civil war. I hope I am patriotic, and I mean to be a good citizen. And let me ask, historically following the march of our nation with her long line of martyrs and heroes, in what age of the world fuller of great thoughts and great deeds could one have lived than in that between 1812 and 1876?

KINSMAN ATKINSON.

OUR respected classmate sends the following interesting and typical account of the life and struggles of a New England boy in the early part of the present century.

I was born in Buxton, Maine, then part of Massachusetts, Oct. 16, 1807, being one of the twelve children of John and Olive (Haley) Atkinson.

As a sort of premonition of my future profession, my elder brothers and their playmates nicknamed me "Elder" or "Old Elder," and setting me on a box or chair required me to *preach* for their amusement.

When I was about five years old, the war of 1812 broke out, and my eldest brother enlisted as a privateer, was taken and imprisoned in Halifax. He was exchanged just in time to prevent his being sent to England. To prevent his going to sea and to furnish work for his large family, my father exchanged his smaller farm in Buxton for two hundred acres of land in Eaton, N. H. My eldest brother was to have one hundred acres for a farm, and he immediately commenced felling the trees and clearing it up.

There was no meeting-house nor settled minister in the town. The school district in which we lived was large in territory. The school-house was on a high hill, about two miles distant, where a school was kept about two or three months in summer and the same in winter. At an early age I was sent to this school in summer, then taught by Miss Delia Danforth. The seats were long benches, without supports for the back. The girls sat on one end, the boys on the other. Once I happened to be sitting nearest the girls, of whom I manifested a shyness. Miss Danforth told me to sit nearer; I hitched an inch or two; that did not satisfy her; so she made me hitch again and again for her amusement. I have no recollection of going to more than one summer school; as soon as I could be of use on the farm my school privileges were limited to the winter.

When twelve years of age, I thought it time to look out for myself, as my father had neither the means to educate me nor to give me a settlement when of age. Therefore, I agreed to live with my brother-in-law till of age, for one hundred and fifty dollars. He purchased one hundred acres of an almost unbroken forest of large extent, the haunt of bears and other wild animals, and gave me my choice between this lot of land and one hundred and fifty dollars if I lived with him till twenty-one years of age.

At fifteen, however, I left him, and went to live with my own brother, then married, and subsequently was obliged to work a year or two gratis for my father as a minor. My school privileges while with my brother amounted to almost nothing; but I was brought more into contact with the world. At eighteen years of age I began to work for myself on small pay. I expended my wages for books, clothing, and nine weeks' schooling at Fryeburg Academy.

In the fall of 1826, being almost nineteen years of age, I left Eaton and all my relations, in a stage coach, with all my effects in a wooden trunk, which I carried on my shoulder from one hotel to another, to go to New Hampton Academy, only twenty-five miles distant. As the stage did not pass through New Hampton, I was accidentally carried beyond it, and when I reached the town of Atkinson, finding an Academy there, I determined to become a member of it. Here I found kind friends, and had much interesting experience, especially in regard to my spiritual affairs, which resulted in my making a public profession of religion before the church and society of the town, feeling irresistibly impelled to offer a broken but excited prayer between the close of the services and the benediction, much to the surprise of the clergyman and the congregation. The effect was indescribable. Some wept aloud. The Holy Spirit seemed to fall on the meeting. The effect on me was that I had the witness of the Spirit to my conversion.

Afterwards, I went to Andover, fitted for college, and entered Bowdoin in 1831. In 1833 I came to Cambridge, graduating in 1834. I studied Theology at Andover, and was ordained a Congregational minister in 1838. I joined the Methodist Conference in 1843, of which I am now a member.

During my preparatory, college and professional studies, I taught nine different schools to defray expenses. I preached four years in the Congregational churches of Mendon and Washington, and subsequently in the Methodist churches of Belchertown, Winchendon, Princeton, Weston, Farnumville, Topsfield, Dedham, Ludlow, and Hubbardstown. I married in 1838 Dorothy Myrick Woods, niece of Rev. Leonard Woods, of Andover, and have had ten children, five of whom are living.

HENRY BLANCHARD.

THE subject of this notice, son of Joseph and Sarah (Brown) Blanchard, was born in Billerica, Mass., Sept. 25, 1811. His father was a farmer, and one of a large family of French origin, who settled in various parts of New England and New York. His maternal grandfather, Benjamin Brown, of Tewksbury, Mass., was a deputy to the first Continental Congress, and an officer in the war of the Revolution.

He remained at home till near the age of seventeen, assisting in such light work as was suitable to his age, attending district schools and such private schools as the town afforded; he was also sent to the Billerica Academy for several terms, where he began the study of Latin and Greek with a view to a collegiate education. About August 1, 1828, he was placed in Phillips Academy, Andover, to commence in earnest his preparation for college.

His father died soon after he left the paternal roof. He was then for the first time called to realize that he had got to depend on his own efforts in his onward way in life. He found himself left with the very inconsiderable patrimony of eight hundred and fifty dollars, with which to make preparation for college, to support himself while there and while studying a profession. After two years' stay at Andover he entered Harvard, being the only one of a class of twenty to enter that college, the rest going to various other colleges which were under Orthodox influences. His father's family all entertained liberal or Unitarian views of Christian belief. At the academy he stood alone in his inherited faith. A very large proportion of all the members of the school belonged to the different evangelical churches and their aim was the ministry. He was, of course, subject to a strong pressure of Orthodox influence, and at an age when a young man is supposed to be somewhat impressible. Instead of yielding quietly to the forces brought to bear against him, he was moved to an earnest effort to stand his ground and hold the fort against all assaults. It cost him somewhat of a struggle, yet it is doubtful if he regretted the ordeal to which he was subjected.

Little is to be said about his college life and success. The two impediments to a more complete realization of what college life ought to be and of the anticipations he had entertained, were his narrow pecuniary circumstances and a constitutional diffidence. As he looks back to those seemingly far off days and sadly calls to mind the difficulties under which he labored from over-sensitiveness and too much distrust of himself, he can imagine how nearly equivalent is plenty of assurance and self-confidence to the actual possession of those facilities which wealth affords.

His stinted means having been hinted at, it may be proper to allude to some of the ways adopted to supply deficiencies. As to beneficiary aid, besides the lack of studiousness and brilliancy of scholarship, his modesty was an obstacle to his success in obtaining much from that source.

As was the custom fifty years ago more than at present, undergraduates availed themselves of the long winter vacation to teach in country district schools. This he did in two successive winters. During two summer vacations he was employed by Dr. Thaddeus W. Harris to assist him in various ways in the College Library. During ten weeks of summer of the Junior year, including the vacation, he was employed at Derry, N. H., to assist Master Hildreth of the Pinkerton Academy in preparing a class of boys for entrance to college.

One summer vacation only was in any degree devoted to recreation. This was partially spent in the country at the paternal homestead. Thus it will appear that college life afforded him but little pastime.

Of incidents in college life personal to himself, few, if any, were enough out of the ordinary routine to call for mention. It may, however, be proper to allude to the fact that each student is likely in the course of his career to manifest a taste or preference for some special branch of study, and will gain a corresponding proficiency in it. This was his case. Of the ancient languages his leaning was very decidedly to the Greek; accordingly his proficiency in that language was fairly commendable. This was fortunate, as he was called upon to teach it much of the time for the three years after graduating. The more he taught and studied it, the more he came to appreciate its richness, expressiveness, and beauty. Of the modern languages his partiality was for the German. It is not unlikely that his love of this language was intensified by his reverential regard for that great, good and learned man, Dr. Follen, his teacher.

To those of his classmates whom he well knew, he formed an attachment; to none did he ever feel an antipathy. This class attachment continues, as well as a thorough loyalty to all the class traditions.

Of tender recollections may be mentioned one incident. When he was settling his last college bills he found a deficiency in his immediately available funds. The circumstance somehow reached the ear of a classmate, "*stat nominis umbra*," who hastened to proffer the loan of more than was required. The accommodation was no more gratefully received than cheerfully offered. It has been a pleasure to him to know that this kindly impulse only foreshadowed a record of generous deeds, which he doubts not "have blessed not less him who gave than those who received."

Fifty years ago he left Alma Mater with some regrets for time misemployed, yet with a conscience tolerably clear. His first essay was, in compliance with the request of one of his tutors, to go to the eastern shore of Maryland to take charge of a private school. This was not with a very ambitious aim from a pecuniary standpoint, but the year there passed was a very enjoyable one. He had an opportunity to view slavery,—not in its most hideous phases,—but he saw enough of its atrocities to enlist his sympathies in the movement, then in its early stages, which culminated in the civil war and its final overthrow.

Returning from the south at the end of a year, he at once accepted a position which was in waiting for him, viz., the charge of the Academy at Hallowell, Me. Here he also spent one year, with better financial results than the preceding. He had mentally decided to prepare himself for the practice of medicine, and felt that it was time to make a beginning. Feeling the need of more means in furtherance of his aim, at the request of citizens of his native town he then opened a private school, and also began his medical studies under the direction of Dr. Zadock Howe, then the most eminent physician and surgeon in Middlesex County. Passing one year in this way, he went to Boston and entered the office of the late George B. Doane, with whom he remained two years, meanwhile attending all the required lectures, hospital clinics, &c., and received his degree of M.D. in the spring of 1840.

Here again his impecuniousness influenced him to his disadvantage. It did not require strong solicitation to induce him to accept an invitation to settle in a somewhat remote country town, Marshfield, Mass., where he had little difficulty in entering upon a tolerably extensive, if not profitable, practice. During his residence here of about twenty years his patrons, in their good will, bestowed on him such offices as were not incompatible with his professional duties. He served much of the time on the School Committee, and in 1858 was elected to represent the district in the Legislature.

He married, June 6, 1841, Sarah C. Farmer, daughter of Jeremiah Farmer, of Billerica, and a direct descendant of Edward Farmer, who came to New England about the year 1670, and settled in Billerica. She is still living, as are also his two sons and two daughters.

In 1861, thinking his children had need of greater educational and social advantages than were attainable in Marshfield, he removed to Dorchester. He also hoped by the change to be enabled to look better after the welfare of those dependent upon him, as well as to make provision for his own later years. By the change, as compared with his former field of service, his labors and responsibilities have been lightened, his intercourse with his professional brethren has been more frequent and of wider extent, as well as more pleasant and profitable.

Such is a brief review of the career of one who for more than fifty years has conscientiously given himself to the duty before him; and though marked by no brilliant results, and unattended by any specially noteworthy events, he trusts it can scarcely be regarded as an idle or wholly useless life. That more should have been achieved, he admits. There must be humble workers as well as brilliant organizers.

In conclusion he cheerfully acknowledges that, in spite of adverse circumstances and embarrassments, in the retrospect he is fully conscious of an experience of many of the so-called blessings of life.

EDWARD DARLEY BOIT.

THE compiler has received the following interesting statement from our classmate, under date of

NEWPORT, March 7, 1884.

My father's name was John Boit. He was born in Boston in 1769, and, with a short interval, went to sea all his life. He was chief officer of the ship Columbia when she gave her name to the great river of that name, and I have been told that when in command of a boat searching for water, was actually the first to discover and enter it.

In 1794 he sailed from Newport in the sloop Union, of ninety-five tons, on a voyage round the world. He went out round Cape Horn, and returned by the Cape of Good Hope, reaching Boston in rather less than two years. His journal says, "she was probably the first sloop that ever circumnavigated the globe," and I believe we may add, "she was the last!" He died in 1828.

My mother's maiden name was Ellen M. Jones, of Newport. When a girl she knew Malbone, the celebrated painter, and we have a miniature of her done by him on ivory, and she is said also to be represented as the "Present" in his picture of the "Present, Past, and Future." She died in 1830.

I have had five sisters and one brother, all dead except my youngest sister, who married Russell Sturgis, of London, where they now live.

I was born in Boston, Aug. 31, 1813. I entered the fourth class at the Boston Latin School in 1825, and remained there until 1828, when, on the death of my father, I was taken from school and put into a store. The next year, however, I resumed my studies, was admitted to Harvard College in 1830, and staid the four years. After leaving college I worked on the survey of Boston Harbor, then being made by Col. Loammi Baldwin.

In the spring of 1836 I made a voyage to Java and Calcutta, and arrived home about the end of the year. The commercial crisis of 1837 prevented another voyage, and, after a time, I became treasurer's clerk of a corporation in State Street.

In February, 1838, I was engaged to Miss Jane P. Hubbard, daughter of the late John Hubbard, of Boston, and we were married June 13, 1839. After my marriage I ran a paper mill, and subsequently entered the Dane Law School at Cambridge, where I went through the usual course of study. I completed my studies in the office of C. P. & B. R. Curtis, in Boston, and on my admission to the bar became their junior partner.

In 1848 I removed with my family to Jamaica Plain, where we lived several years. While there I represented West Roxbury, of which Jamaica Plain formed a part, for two years in the Massachusetts Legislature. About 1854 I partially agreed with a lawyer in Chicago to join him as a conveyancer there. I worked on the details for nearly a year; then abandoned the project, and sold out my interest in the books to my intended partner.

Still later I retired from the law, and was made treasurer of the Newton Mills, a cotton factory near Boston. About 1860, in connection with a capitalist, I superintended the building of the Oriental Mills, another cotton factory, near Providence, R. I., of which, when completed, I became treasurer. We subsequently built the Oriental Point Works, ten miles from Providence, and I was made treasurer of them also.

In 1868 I resigned these positions, and established a cotton commission at Savannah, Ga.; but the enterprise was not successful, and in 1875 I returned to Boston, and have not engaged in active business since. During our residence in Savannah, Mrs. Boit and I made two trips to Europe. We visited England, Scotland, France and Italy, but did not make a general tour of the continent. We came back from our last visit in 1875, and settled at Newport, where we now live. We have had six children, three boys and three girls. Of these, the youngest died in infancy, and in 1875, while abroad, we lost our eldest daughter, Elizabeth Greene, widow of Joseph H. Patten, of Providence (who died a few months before her), and their deaths constitute the one great sorrow of an otherwise almost uninterrupted domestic happiness of forty-six years. Our surviving daughter, Jane H., is now Mrs. Arthur Hunnewell, of Boston.

Our eldest son. Edward D., graduated from Harvard in 1863. He was admitted to the bar, but did not practise. In 1864 he married Miss L. M. Cushing, of Watertown. He is an artist, and has lived abroad many years, where he now is.

Our second son, Robert A., graduated in 1868. He went with us to Savannah, and there married Miss Georgie Mercer, who has since deceased, leaving two little girls. He is engaged in the insurance business in Boston. Our youngest son, John, is an architect, and lives with us at Newport.

As for myself, in theology I am a Unitarian; in politics a conservative Democrat, and an advocate of civil service reform and free trade. I am also a total abstainer from the use of alcohol and tobacco.

I begin what some one calls "the march along the melancholy line of the Seventies," strong in faith and hope, and expecting to die firm in the conviction that "Life is indeed worth living."

HENRY BURROUGHS.

HENRY BURROUGHS, the only child of Henry and Catherine (Greene) Burroughs, was born in Boston, April 18, 1815. His mother died when he was two years old, and his home during his childhood and youth was at the family mansion in Hollis Street, covering with its garden the site now called Burroughs Place.

From 1823 to 1830 he was a scholar in the celebrated academy of Mr. Charles W. Greene (H. C. 1802), at Jamaica Plain, where he was prepared for Harvard College, entering in 1830 at the age of fifteen. After leaving college he devoted a year to general study in Boston, and in 1835 entered the General Theological Seminary of the Protestant Episcopal Church in the city of New York. Having completed the course of study in that institution and received the usual testimonials, he was ordained Deacon by the Rt. Rev. Dr. Griswold, Bishop of the Eastern Diocese, in Trinity Church, Boston, on the 15th of July, 1838. He soon afterwards entered upon the charge of St. Paul's Church, Camden, Trinity Church, Moorestown, and St. Mary's Church, Colestown, New Jersey. He was married in Trinity Church, Boston, December 18, 1838, to Miss Sarah Tilden, daughter of the late William Tilden, and granddaughter of Captain George Inman of the British army. He was admitted to the priesthood by the Rt. Rev. George W. Doane, Bishop of New Jersey, in St. Mary's Church, Burlington, N. J., May 29, 1839. After a residence of five years at Camden, he removed to Massachusetts, and became rector of St. John's Church in the beautiful village of Northampton, where he lived from 1843 to 1852. He then removed to Boston with his family, and resided twenty-nine years, during all which time he was engaged in the duties of the ministry. After officiating in St. Paul's Church, Brookline, for a few months, he had the temporary charge of Grace Church, Providence, R. I., in 1853 and 1854. In 1855 and 1856 he acted as assistant minister in St. John's Church, Portsmouth, N. H., during the illness of his uncle, the Rev. Charles Burroughs, D.D. He then assumed the pastoral care of St. Mary's Church, Newton Lower Falls, which he held for about two years. From 1860 to 1868, he was rector of Christ Church, Quincy, and in October, 1868, he became Rector of Christ Church, Boston, which office he held till July, 1881, when he sailed for England, and was absent till December, 1883.

On the 28th of December, 1873, he delivered an address, which was afterwards published, on the one hundred and fiftieth anniversary of the opening of Christ Church, the oldest house of worship in Boston; and on the 18th of April, 1875, he held in the church a service commemorating the hanging out of Paul Revere's signal lanterns from the tower of Christ Church on the night before the battle of Lexington. He served fourteen years on the School Committee of the city of Boston, and was for ten years the Chairman of the Committee on the Girls' High and Normal School. He was for several years Secretary of the Standing Committee of the Diocese of Massachusetts from 1873 to 1881, the Boston Episcopal Charitable Society from 1855 to 1871, the Widows' and Orphans' Society from 1865 to 1881, and of other institutions. He has also for ten years held the position of Examining Chaplain to the Bishop of Massachusetts. The degree of S.T.D. was conferred upon him by Trinity College, Hartford, in 1876.

His oldest son, Major George Burroughs, graduated at West Point in 1862, and received two brevets for meritorious services as an officer of the Corps of Engineers during the war of the rebellion. He died while on duty in the harbor of Charleston, S. C., January 22, 1870.

His second son, Henry, died on the 9th of October, 1882, at Southsea, England.

His only daughter, Catharine, was married to Dr. Luther Parks, of Boston, and is now residing in Europe.

JAMES FREEMAN COLMAN.

By Mr. Colman's request, all notice of him is omitted.

BENJAMIN EDDY COTTING.

THIS sketch of the life of our classmate is taken mainly from the Biographical Encyclopædia of Massachusetts.—T. C.

Benjamin Eddy Cotting, son of William and Sarah (Eddy) Cotting, was born in West Cambridge, now Arlington, Mass., November 2, 1812.

In early life young Cotting's inclinations were for the military service, and his education was of the special character required to fit him for the National Military Academy. Before the design could be consummated, other considerations interfered, and the purpose was abandoned. After studying in his native town he entered Harvard University without conditions in 1830. There he received some of the highest testimonials to the excellence of his scholarship in the exhibition appointments of his class, and graduated with honors in 1834.

In the third year of his college course he undertook the temporary charge of an academy at North Andover, and bore with tact and success the inevitable trials of temper and abilities that usually attend a first essay at teaching. After receiving his diploma he deliberately chose the healing art as the calling to which his energies should be devoted. He studied at the Harvard Medical School, which then enjoyed the teachings of professors so eminent in the profession, as Warren, Jackson, Bigelow, Hayward, and Ware," and took his degree in 1837.

School instruction was supplemented by service as *interne* at the County House of Industry,—an institution then affording special and highly appreciated opportunities for clinical observation. Many discomforts accompanied his labors there. The officers of the establishment showed slight consideration for medical assistants. But his zeal and persistent thirst for knowledge overcame official prejudices, and bore him triumphantly through.

Dr. Cotting remained for a while in Boston, supplementing his work as a physician by giving instruction in the classics and mathematics, in which he was a proficient. Twenty-five physicians, of whom he was the last comer, then occupied Winter Street, in the heart of the city. One after the other, all were driven out by the onward advance of trade, and sought residences in other parts of the city or neighborhood. Acting under the advice of judicious medical friends, in 1843 he removed to Roxbury, then an independent township. There he speedily achieved surprising and exceptional success. Physicians and citizens were familiarized with his unusual surgical aptitude. Quick to seize and patient to improve the fitting opportunity, successful management of critical surgical cases spread abroad his fame through all that neighborhood. Up to recent years he performed most of the unusual as well as ordinary surgical operations in Roxbury and vicinity. Reputation widened as experience increased, and won for him the position he now holds on the consulting staff of the Boston City Hospital. He had previously several times declined the office of attending surgeon at the Hospital.

In the public affairs of Roxbury, Dr. Cotting exhibited keen and abiding interest so long as it remained an independent municipality. As one of the trustees of the Roxbury Latin School for many years, he gave much attention to its management. He resisted the prevailing tendency to extravagance in expensive schoolhouses; and with another trustee he planned and erected an inexpensive building, the only one in the neighborhood that cost less than the appropriations, and one which still remains unsurpassed in completeness for the purposes intended. For eight years he served as physician to the Roxbury Almshouse;— a connection which afforded exceptional opportunities for medical observation. More than two thousand cases came under his notice in that institution alone. A first class hospital rarely offers to an individual practitioner a larger number or a greater pathological diversity within a similar period.

In 1837 Dr. Cotting was admitted to the fellowship of the

Massachusetts Medical Society, and has since manifested an earnest and consistent devotion to its interests and purposes. Never passive or indifferent, but always active and vigorous in relation to that institution and to the medical profession as a whole, he has labored with diligence unexcelled by any of his compeers, to raise and to maintain a high standard of professional morality and discipline in his ancestral state. Whether as officer of the Society or as private member of its ranks, by word, act, and influence, he has evinced the truest appreciation of the regular medical profession of Massachusetts.

Nor has the profession failed to recognize his personal merit and the value of his professional services. In 1853 he was selected to represent the Norfolk District in the Council of the Massachusetts Medical Society. With the single exception of the year 1865, in which he was absent from the country, he has ever since been one of the Councillors, and has wielded potential influence in shaping the policy and perfecting the organization of the Society. In 1855 he was chosen Recording Secretary, and in 1857 Corresponding Secretary of that institution. To the latter office he was reëlected annually until 1865, in which year he was chosen to deliver the annual discourse. That duty was accomplished in a manner that still lives in the memory of those who heard the address. In 1872 he was elected Vice-President. In that position Dr. Cotting created so favorable an opinion by his enterprise and wisdom in fostering the interests of the Society, that its members departed from the usage established by half a century of precedents, and made him President in 1874. So effective did his administration prove, that the Society has since dated its new departure on a career of harmonious prosperity and efficient work from that epoch. The debt of the association was liquidated. New life was infused into the various district societies by the periodical visitation of the President,—an innovation of his own initiation; the social needs of the profession were provided for, and a special fund*

---

* Dr. Cotting has given to the Massachusetts Medical Society a fund of $2,000, the income of which is devoted to providing a lunch for the Councillors at each of their stated meetings, annually, for which, no doubt, his name will be held in grateful remembrance.—T. C.

was created by his liberality for the continuance of that provision. Generous gifts of money for prizes and other purposes, personal activity in important special and standing committees, unabated interest in all matters of whatever magnitude, affecting the honor and welfare of his medical brethren in Massachusetts, richly entitle him to their gratitude and respect.

Outside the State society, Dr. Cotting's affiliations with medical and scientific bodies are quite numerous. He is a Fellow and also a Councillor of the American Academy of Arts and Sciences; an honorary member of the Connecticut and of the New Hampshire State Medical Societies; a corresponding member of the Royal Medical Society of Athens, Greece,[*] and of the Academia de' Quiriti at Rome.

The Obstetrical Society of Boston, the Norfolk District Society, and the Boston Society for Medical Improvement, owe much to his zeal and labor in founding and maintaining them.

When, in 1843, his friend Dr. Jeffries Wyman retired from the office of Curator of the Lowell Institute in Boston, Dr. Cotting became his successor. Sound judgment and ready tact, together with the expenditure of much time, are demanded by its duties. The promptitude and fulness with which the requisition has been satisfied have been largely compensated by the intimate relation it involves with many eminent scientists and scholars. Acquaintance thus began with Agassiz, Guyot, Lyell and others,—acquaintance which ripened into valued and permanent friendship.

The activity of Dr. Cotting's life is apparent in this necessarily brief biographic sketch. It would not admit of elegant leisure. Extensive and engrossing practice afforded no respite. Only by breaking away from ever increasing local engagements could he obtain an occasional rest. In 1848 he visited Europe, and witnessed some of the stirring scenes connected with the deposition of Louis Phillippe and the promulgation of the French Republic. Again, in 1860, he made an extended European tour, in which Constantinople and the city of Athens

[*] He replied to the Royal Medical Society of Athens, in Greek, accepting the membership which had been bestowed upon him by vote of the Society, showing that the teachings of his Alma Mater had fallen on good soil.—T. C.

were included. Again, in 1865, he crossed the Atlantic for the purpose of recreation in travel. The immediate need of the last trip was occasioned by his exposure to unfavorable climatic influences while an efficient member of Prof. Agassiz's exploring expedition to Brazil. Physical disturbances peculiar to the tropics, and from the effects of which he has never fully recovered, compelled him to leave the distinguished company somewhat sooner than he intended, and to seek a more genial climate. While in Brazil he was introduced to the enlightened and patriotic Emperor, Dom Pedro, and thus began an acquaintance which his Majesty spontaneously renewed during his recent visit to the United States.

In addition to frequent contributions to periodical medical literature, Dr. Cotting has written three more formal productions on medical topics. The first is an address entitled "Nature in Disease," which was delivered in May, 1832; the second, an address entitled "Disease, a part of the Plan of Creation," delivered in 1865, at the annual meeting of the Massachusetts Medical Society, which attracted great attention. The more liberal of medical thinkers received it cordially, although it has not escaped criticism of a less friendly nature. In 1866 it received the compliment of translation and publication in the French language in Paris. The last of the addresses referred to was delivered in May, 1872, under the title of "My First Question as a Medical Student—its Solution a sure Basis for Rational Therapeutics."

Each of these essays is a plea for rational medical science and procedure; each is a protest against perturbation—against empirical and unnecessary medication. All were republished by the author in 1875, in a small volume bearing the title of "Medical Addresses for gratuitous distribution, especially to the Fellows of the Massachusetts Medical Society."

Dr. Cotting married, Oct. 5, 1843, at Brooklyn, N. Y., Miss Catharine Greene Sayer, born at Dedham, Mass., of New England origin. Accompanying him on a journey to California, she died of painless pneumonia, April 29, 1881, in a railroad-car, as the train was nearing the "1,000 mile tree" in Utah Territory, with prairie flowers in her hand, while uttering the words "beautiful, grand," as her eyes caught sight of the snow-covered summits of Pike's Peak; a circumstance which excited the deep sympathy of the many friends of herself and husband. She left no children.

Dr. Cotting has always felt great interest in everything pertaining to the class of 1834, which he has shown in many substantial ways.

THOMAS CUSHING.

HAVING tried in vain to get a notice of myself written by another hand, I propose to do it with the freedom and frankness which I have enjoined with some degree of success upon others, as being the proper thing among classmates.

I was born in Bulfinch Place, Boston, April 10, 1814, being the oldest son of Thomas and Eliza Constantia (Watson) Cushing. When I say that I am the ninth in descent on both sides from Plymouth pilgrims, I think I need not go any farther back in regard to my ancestors. When I was four years old, mercantile vicissitudes compelled a change from the liberal and pleasant surroundings in which I was born to a comparatively humbler residence in the neighboring rural village of Dorchester, where I learned something of country life as well as sufficient book knowledge in the schools of the town to enable me to enter the Public Latin School at the age of ten years, when I had again become an inhabitant of Boston.

The Latin School, during my five years of attendance, was in a very high state of efficiency and popularity under B. A. Gould (H. C. 1814) and F. P. Leverett (H. C. 1821) as principals, and E. S. Dixwell (H. C. 1827) as sub-master,* and

---

* Subsequently principal, 1836-1851.

several gentlemen as teachers, who afterwards became distinguished in their various professions. It embraced nearly all the boys in the city who were aiming at an extended or university education, about two hundred and fifty in number, with just as much distinction of class and means as it is wholesome for boys to be brought up under. And here let me record my happy and satisfactory recollections of the years that I passed at this school. Everything is fixed in my memory in the brightest and rosiest colors. My teachers were eminently gentlemen and scholars, my associates agreeable to me, the discipline strict but not cruel, the short and decisive methods of which were never applied to me without the consciousness, on my part, that they were richly deserved, and that they cleared the score for me for the time being, leaving no sting to break my sleep or interrupt my play. My country training and sturdy frame enabled my right hand to keep my head and maintain my rights out of doors, a somewhat necessary accomplishment in those days. The long school year and school days, equivalent to nearly double in amount of school hours to the present ever-shrinking allowance, enabled us to do our work without hurrying or undue pressure, and, in fact, to do much more than was necessary to enter college, which, again, was by no means so little as is sometimes assumed now-a-days. For its purpose and in its day, I do not hesitate to say, having some knowledge of schools, that the Latin School at that time was of almost ideal excellence, and that I gained there what was of inestimable advantage to me in my college course and future pursuits.

The fame of the thorough and elegant scholarship of Robert C. Winthrop and George S. Hillard was still alive in the school, and among my schoolmates were Charles Sumner, Lothrop Motley, James Freeman Clarke, William M. Evarts, Wendell Phillips, Henry W. Torrey, and many others who have obtained distinction in life and shown that the school was building upon a sure foundation of classical and mathematical culture.

I had such confidence also in my teachers that I felt that whatever they said was right and whatever they required was possible, and therefore to be done without hesitation or grumbling. This was strikingly exemplified by the readiness with which I undertook the writing of a so-called Greek poem for my graduating exercise, at rather short notice. Though I had never written a line of Greek or made a Greek letter except for amusement, I never thought of pleading inability, but by diligent plying of Lexicon and Gradus, early and late, during the hot mid-August days, in due time I turned out the required forty lines, which could be scanned, and I flattered myself had the true Homeric ring to them. I have thus always had the pleasure of looking back upon the school portion of my life, which to many is not an agreeable subject of reflection, with feelings of unalloyed pleasure and happiness. As illustrating this, I find on the blank leaf of my well-thumbed old Greek grammar, under date of Aug. 20, 1829 :—

"My last day at Latin School.
Sorry to leave it."

Not much poetry or sentiment in this, but a boy's downright expression of an honest conviction.

After quitting school in 1829, the "*res angusta domi*" made my prospect of a more extended education rather misty; but just at the time when it was necessary for me to take some step as to my future support, my fate was fixed and my life-work settled by a casual meeting with another of my teachers, whose memory I can never sufficiently honor, Mr. Gideon F. Thayer, whose intermediate school I had attended, as was quite the custom in those days, at the noon hours, for instruction in some of the English branches not taught in the Latin School. Mr. Thayer finding my course undecided, proposed to me to commence the work of teaching in its simplest elements, as an apprentice to the business, in the new private institution, Chauncy-Hall School, which he had just founded in Boston, and where there was plenty of work for every capacity. He offered me also the opportunity to continue my studies in any of the departments of the school. This offer I was glad to accept, and in September, 1829, I began my work, little thinking that I was to carry it on in the same institution, with a comparatively short intermission, for just half a century.

The hope of a collegiate education was not entirely abandoned, and my studies were mostly turned in that direction, in the hope of some day rejoining my old Latin-School classmates by entering a year or more in advance. This hope was sufficiently strong to induce me at the age of sixteen to supplement a long day's work in the school, of seven hours at least, with so much study in the early morning or late evening as enabled me, though without a teacher, to keep up with the class that entered Harvard in 1830, until the door was unexpectedly opened for me to join it in the January of 1832, by the kind offices of one who made it her pleasure to assist those striving to obtain a collegiate education. My habits of early study and power of long and continuous labor, with perfect health and a thorough preparation, made college work seem very light to me, and I was able to do considerable towards my own support by giving private instruction and assisting Mr. Sparks in arranging and copying the Washington manuscripts for the press; and all this without neglecting my own studies or cutting myself off from the athletic and social pleasures of college life, which I enjoyed like one long holiday, though I voluntarily practised what seem in the retrospect severe economies, and always graduated my expenditures by my means.

I think myself and classmates to have been fortunate in having been members of the college just when we were. The recent accession of Mr. Quincy to the presidency had given a wholesome stir and impulse to the institution as a whole, while the classical and modern language departments had received a decided advance from such eminent scholars as Drs. Beck and Follen. The rhetorical department, as administered by Dr. Edward T. Channing, was at the height of its usefulness. The studies pursued with him were the most interesting part of my work, and I can never be sufficiently thankful for the very liberal allowance of work demanded of us, and the pains that he took to ground us in the writing of correct English and in forming some idea of proper style and expression. If, as I have understood, this department is now less prominent and less work is done in it, the more's the pity.

I took much pleasure also in the exercises of the Harvard Washington Corps, then in a very flourishing condition, and was happy to fill several of the humbler positions, requiring considerable labor and responsibility, though not conspicuous in the eyes of our fair friends on Exhibition Days.

The athletic exercises of the students were on a pleasant and comfortable footing. They were not made a business of, nor entrusted to nines or elevens. Anybody could participate in football, cricket, etc., as then played, who had a reasonable modicum of strength and hardihood, and large numbers did so at their leisure moments, much to their own advantage. Swimming in the noble Charles was also a recreation very largely indulged in, as the summer term lasted nearly through July. All these things were strictly amusements, and were therefore pleasurable and profitable, and did not interfere at all with serious work.

A little cloud was thrown over the end of our Senior year, which it is not necessary to speak of more particularly. Otherwise my college life was a time of unalloyed satisfaction, of which, as of my school days, I was sorry to see the end. I had succeeded in obtaining what had been the chief object of my youthful ambition, which of itself was enough to make me happy.

If I am considered too much of an optimist in these recollections, and of seeing things too much *couleur de rose*, if it is thought that I ought to be able to conjure up some shadows for my picture, it probably grows out of the fact that I lived in such a state of exuberant health and strength that life itself was a pleasure to me, that I almost grudged a little time for sleep, and was always ready and happy to face the new day with its labors, trials, and responsibilities.

But college life came to an end, and having duly "graduated," in September, 1834, I took the place that was ready for me at Chauncy-Hall School, succeeding Mr. Henry W. Pickering (H. C. 1831) as sole instructor of the Classical Department.

The scope of this paper will not permit me to give any detailed account of my life as a teacher. Suffice it to say that in the various capacities of instructor, junior partner, sole proprietor and principal, and senior partner, I was uninterruptedly connected with the school till July, 1879, which time I had previously set for my retirement (somewhat jocosely at first, as it seemed so far off), as fifty years from the time of my beginning my apprenticeship. But it *did* come, and though it found me perfectly well and able to go on with my work, I deemed it best to do what I had deliberately decided to be most judicious, and retire when I was still able to enjoy life and perhaps make myself slightly useful, rather than wait till I was compelled to leave my post by ill-health or failing powers.

I will only say further, that for more than thirty years I did all the work of the classical department and a good deal in others, besides all the multifarious duties of one of the principals of a large private school, averaging about two hundred pupils; that while I was connected with it, between four and five thousand pupils passed, metaphorically, *sub ferulâ*, while at least two hundred were prepared for different colleges, mostly for Harvard.

It will hardly be esteemed arrogant, I trust, to assume that there must have been some reason other than chance at the bottom of the steady success of a private school for more than half a century. If asked to put this in the fewest possible words, I should say it was the application from the start of common sense and hard work. There was no pretence of any wonderful system that would place scholars on an equality and do away with the necessity of brains and labor. The gates of any "royal road" to learning did not open through that building. Nobody's opinions were allowed to come between the teacher and pupil in matters of instruction or discipline. No profession of making the acquisition of knowledge particularly easy was ever held out; but the pupils were guided into the ways of wholesome labor and orderly conduct, and held there by a strict and steady discipline. Those who did not like these conditions were welcome to go elsewhere.

Working thus untrammeled and irresponsible, except to my own conscience, I was always comfortable and happy in my position, and can say with truth that I enjoyed my fifty years of school-keeping, and still enjoy the retrospect of it. That I was able to do this under the very heavy burden of work that for a large portion of the time was laid upon my shoulders, arose no doubt from the fact that they were made broad and strong enough to bear it by the uninterrupted continuance of perfect health and great endurance; for without these the lot of the teacher must be truly miserable. Fortunately my tastes helped to keep up this state of things. I was fond of and practised regularly athletic exercises, such as boxing, fencing, gymnastics, and, as I grew older, riding, adding to the good results of the last exercise by using horses hard-trotting enough to stir the blood in the coldest winter weather. I have also been mildly, but usually unsuccessfully, addicted to field-sports; but have had what I consider the chief advantage of them, air, exercise, and something to turn the mind out of its usual course of thought. It is probably owing to unsuitable original conditions and the want of taste for out-of-door exercises and pursuits, that school-keeping is so often distasteful and injurious to the health.

When I began to teach, the summer vacation was about two and a half weeks in length, and the problem of how to pass it was pretty simple. But after it had gradually expanded to the whole month of August, and I began to have a young family growing up around me, I thought it best to secure a little spot of mother earth, where, far from fashion and its votaries and the ways of hotels and boarding-houses, I could build a shelter, at least, before all the beautiful spots were taken possession of for the summer mansions of the rich. I found such a place on a beautiful beach in the town of North Scituate, Mass., and having found an optimistic Yankee carpenter, who promised " to build me a palace for five hundred dollars," I allowed him to do so. Here I have had my summer residence since 1848, with great advantage to myself and family, who have all become in a measure boatmen, fishermen, and farmers, besides dabbling in many of the mechanic arts. At first activity was necessary to provide food for a family, and I sometimes told inquiring friends that I lived "like the American Indians, by hunting and fishing." But others have now found out the advantages and beauty of the locality; land has risen from $50 to $2,500 or more an acre, neighbors are crowding upon me, and, were I younger, I would shoulder my gun and seek some more remote place to pass my summers.

I have not attempted to do much outside of my profession, not even to make a school book, finding those in use sufficiently good if properly applied. I was one of the early members of the American Institute of Instruction, a body which took the first steps towards the educational improvements of the last fifty years. I was for many years its secretary, and lectured several times before it and other educational bodies, besides giving my views on practical instruction in the annual school catalogues. I have visited Europe several times in vacations, and spent perhaps the most interesting week of my life in Athens in 1874.

On the 5th of June, 1841, I married Elizabeth Adelaide, daughter of Aaron Baldwin, Esq., of Boston, whose talents and virtues were always a delight and inspiration to me. Her death at about the time of my retirement from the school in 1879, disappointed my hopes of devoting my time to her failing health, which had influenced me in taking that step. She left me four sons, all of whom have been educated at Chauncy-Hall School and Harvard College, and are distributed among the professions. I have also eight grandchildren.

I do not by any means find my time unoccupied since I have retired from active teaching. I have done some amateur work, and am trying gradually to make some impression on the vast mass of interesting reading that I was obliged to put off to a "more convenient season," and which I could not exhaust were I to live a hundred years longer.

Living in my native city among those whom I helped to educate, I meet friends at every turn, young, middle-aged, and even white-haired, and none are more friendly and more ready to acknowledge the benefits of school discipline than those who were the special subjects of it. In my travels, also, the inevitable old pupil turns up, greets me with satisfaction, and usually gives a good account of himself. If I have made any enemies they give no indication of it.

With so much kindness around me and perfect health, I hope to live out gratefully whatever years may be added to the allotted span of life.

FREDERIC DWIGHT.

FREDERIC DWIGHT, son of Jonathan (H. C. 1793) and Sarah (Shepherd) Dwight, was born in Northampton about 1815.

He received his preliminary education at the famous Round-Hill School, of which his brother-in-law, George Bancroft (H. C. 1817) was one of the founders. Mr. Dwight has not furnished any connected account of his life since leaving college, though repeatedly requested to do so, but has sent instead copious philosophical and political speculations, for which there is not room in a publication of this sort.

He has lived a retired life at Agawam, near Springfield, and devoted himself to theoretical and speculative pursuits.

SAMUEL MORSE FELTON.

SAMUEL MORSE FELTON, son of Cornelius Conway and Anna (Morse) Felton, was born at West Newbury, Mass., July 17, 1809. His father early removed to North Chelsea, near Saugus, where the subject of this sketch attended the village school, and passed his spare time in working upon the farms in the neighborhood. When fourteen and a half years old, he entered a grocery store in Boston as errand boy and clerk, where he stayed till eighteen. His older brother, Cornelius Conway (H. C. 1827), having just graduated with high honors, and having been appointed one of the Principals of the Livingston County High School, in New York, he entered that institution as scholar and clerk, staying there two years, and preparing himself for Harvard, which he entered in August, 1830. During his four years' residence in Cambridge, he supported himself by teaching school during vacations, and private pupils during term time. In college he was a member of the Institute of 1770, the Hasty Pudding Club and Phi Beta Kappa Society, and on taking his degree of A.M. in 1837, he had the honor of delivering the Latin Oration.

After leaving Cambridge, he opened a school in Charlestown, and entered his name with Judge Dana, intending to make the law his profession. The confinement was too much for his health, and he soon gave up the law for the more congenial study of Civil Engineering, entering the office of the distinguished engineer, Col. Loammi Baldwin (H. C. 1800). After Col. Baldwin's death in 1838, Mr. Felton opened an office on his own account, made the first survey of the Fresh-Pond Railroad, and built it in 1841. He then surveyed and built the Fitchburg Railroad, of which he was Superintendent and Engineer until 1851, at the same time having been engaged on other New England railroads, notably the Cheshire, Rutland and Burlington and Vermont Central. In 1851 he was appointed president of the Philadelphia, Wilmington and Baltimore Railroad, and removed to Philadelphia, where he has since resided.

The position which he occupied on this railroad, connecting as it does the North with the South, brought him in contact with many men prominent in the two sections of the country then drawing apart for the conflict which was soon to follow.*

---

* An episode in Mr. Felton's experience while president of this road is of such national interest that it is thought best to give it at length.
Early in 1861 it came to his knowledge from rumors that there was a conspir-

In 1865 Mr. Felton was obliged from shattered health to resign the presidency of the Philadelphia, Wilmington and Baltimore Railroad. In October of that year the Pennsylvania Steel

ncy on foot among the southern sympathizers in Baltimore against the railroad of which he had charge. Determined to investigate the truth of these rumors, he took into the employ of the railroad the now celebrated detective, Allan Pinkerton. Pinkerton, with eight assistants, set to work and in a short time unearthed a conspiracy much more widespread and serious than had been supposed. This conspiracy was briefly as follows: if an attempt was made to inaugurate the president-elect in Washington, Mr. Lincoln was to be made way with in Baltimore on his way through that city; if, on the other hand, as then seemed probable, Mr. Lincoln was inaugurated in Philadelphia, and troops were called for the defence of Washington, the bridges on the Philadelphia, Wilmington and Baltimore Railroad, between the Susquehanna River and Baltimore, were to be burned, Washington isolated from the loyal North, and thus handed over to the Southerners, who were to seize it and the national archives and declare themselves *de facto* the national government of the United States. When Mr. Lincoln arrived in Philadelphia, on his way to Washington, his programme was to go from Philadelphia to Harrisburg, where he was to speak, and then make his way to Washington, via the Northern Central Railroad and Baltimore. Immediately on the announcement of this plan, the detectives reported that the attention of the conspirators in Baltimore had been transferred to the Northern Central Railroad, and that Mr. Lincoln would be waylaid and murdered on his approach to Baltimore by that route. On Mr. Lincoln's arrival in Philadelphia, Mr. Felton, through a friend of Mr. Lincoln, acquainted him with the plot against his life, and urged him to go to Washington privately that night. This Mr. Lincoln refused to do, saying that he had promised to speak in Harrisburg, and that he must fulfil his promise; but that after he had done so, he would place himself in the hands of his friends. The following plan was then arranged by Mr. Felton for his safe transmission to Washington. After delivering his address in Harrisburg, he was apparently to retire with Gov. Curtin for the night, but really to be driven to a point two miles outside of Harrisburg, where a special car and engine were to await him, and immediately start with him for Philadelphia. Meanwhile the telegraph wires leading in all directions from Harrisburg were to be cut. The special train conveying Mr. Lincoln of necessity arrived in Philadelphia later than the schedule time for the departure of the night express for Washington. It therefore became necessary to delay this train, and at the same time to give some explanation of its delay to the management of the Baltimore and Ohio Railroad in Baltimore, in asking them to await its arrival before starting their train for Washington. Mr. Felton, therefore, stated to the authorities of the Baltimore and Ohio that he was preparing a very important package of papers for despatch by the night express; that very probably he would have to delay his train for it, and asked the Baltimore and Ohio if they would, as a personal favor to him, delay the departure of their train to Washington until the arrival of his train from Philadelphia. This request was readily complied with. The night express awaited Mr. Lincoln's arrival in Philadelphia, took him to Baltimore, where the train for Washington was awaiting this important package of papers, and took it safely through to the nation's capital, the conspirators in Baltimore meanwhile supposing the president-elect quietly sleeping in Harrisburg. In the morning the first message which came over the wires from Washington was, "Your package has arrived safely and been delivered," the preconcerted signal that all was well, and that treason had been defeated.

After the celebrated passage of the Sixth Massachusetts Volunteers through Baltimore, the plot before contrived against the railroad was carried into effect, the bridges burned and Washington cut off from all communication with the North. During the previous winter the route to Washington via Annapolis had

Company, the first concern to manufacture Bessemer Steel on a commercial scale in the United States, was organized, and Mr. Felton chosen its president, an office which he has held ever since. He has for many years been connected with various railroads of the country, having been director in the Northern Pacific, St. Paul and Duluth, Lehigh Coal and Navigation Co., Delaware Railroad, Eastern Shore, Chester Creek, Ogdensburg and Lake Champlain, Pennsylvania, Reading, West Jersey and Pennsylvania Co. In Gov. Andrew's administration he was appointed a State Commissioner of the Hoosac Tunnel. Later he was one of the five government commissioners appointed to make a final examination of the Union and Central Pacific Railroads. In 1875 and 1876 he was one of the Centennial Board of Finance, which organized and managed the Centennial Exhibition, and is now President of the Harvard Club of Philadelphia.

Mr. Felton has been twice married, and has four daughters and three sons, all living, and nine grandchildren. One of his sons was a graduate of Harvard College, class of 1879; one is a member of the present Sophomore class; and one is a graduate of the Institute of Technology at Boston, and is a civil engineer.

been suggested to Gen. Scott by Mr. Felton in case the bridges were destroyed, and this route was at once organized by Mr. Felton and Mr. J. Edgar Thompson, president of the Pennsylvania Railroad. These two gentlemen, on their own responsibility, hired and provisioned steamers and despatched them to Annapolis and the Susquehanna. Gen. Butler, on his arrival in Philadelphia, found everything arranged for his transmission to Washington viâ Annapolis. At first he refused to go, saying that his orders were to go through Baltimore. But more prudent counsels prevailed, and Butler went to Washington viâ Annapolis, and in a characteristic spirit claimed for himself the credit of having originated and opened what was then the only way of reaching the isolated capital.

HENRY GASSETT.

HENRY GASSETT, son of Henry (H. C. 1795) and Lucy (Wood) Gassett, was born in Boston, February 7, 1813. His father was the great-grandson of a French Huguenot, Henri Gachet, who emigrated from La Rochelle about the year 1700 to Taunton, Mass.

In 1821, after a schooling of several years under Messrs. Greely, Thayer, and others in Boston, he was sent to North Andover to the Franklin Academy, Simeon Putnam (H. C. 1811) Principal. In 1826, at the age of thirteen, he was sent to Paris, where he spent two years at the Pension Rouet. In 1828 he returned to North Andover. Among his schoolmates at North Andover were several who have become more or less distinguished in after life, viz., Oliver Ames, Dr. William Dale, C. C. Felton, John M. Farley, Dr. William Ingalls, Dr. George B. Loring, Amos A. Lawrence, Prof. Benjamin Pierce, Rev. Chandler Robbins, and Rev. J. F. W. Ware.

On leaving college he went into his father's counting-room, and after a business experience of sixteen years, withdrew to country life, cultivating a farm of eighty-six acres in North Wrentham, Mass., now Norfolk. In 1858 he left home for a tour of nearly three years throughout Europe, Egypt and Palestine, returning to his farm in 1861. In 1866 he removed to Dorchester, Mass., and has fully occupied his time since in the care of his place and the management of his own and trust property. In 1884 he removed to Braintree, where he now resides.*

---

* Mr. Gassett upheld alone the cause of music on the part of the very unmusical class of 1834 in the Pierian Sodality; he also was instrumental with John S. Dwight and others in organizing the Harvard Musical Association.—T. C.

HENRY FRANCIS HARRINGTON.

HENRY FRANCIS HARRINGTON, the second son of Joseph and Rebecca (Smith) Harrington, was born in Roxbury, Mass., where his parents lived, August 15, 1814. His early boyhood was quite uneventful, and was passed in his native town. In the fall of 1828, being then fourteen years old, he was sent to Phillips Academy, Exeter, N. H., to be fitted for college. There he remained till he entered college in 1830. He was a mere boy in college—to repeat, by direction, his own statement, and more "interested in mischief" and amusement than in study. Consequently he was but little benefited by his college career, except in the branch of English literature, of which he was extravagantly fond.

He spent the first year after his graduation in Boston as usher in the English High School. Then embracing a favorable opportunity, he became one of the publishers and editors of a newspaper in Boston, a position for which he had an ardent inclination. But the terrible financial prostration of 1837 came on, and just as he had reason to feel that he had successfully weathered the storm, and placed his business on a firm foundation, his overtasked constitution gave way, and for a year or more he lingered, as was supposed, between life and death; then he began to mend.

After a short season of labor in New York city as editor of a monthly periodical, during which time he was studying for the Unitarian ministry, he went south in aid of his health, and preached for several months in Savannah, Georgia.

Returning to the north in the spring of 1841, he was stationed in Providence, R. I., for three years as minister at large, in the service of the Unitarian societies of that city; and then, much preferring to organize new religious societies than to minister to old ones, he founded a society successively in Albany and Troy, N. Y., and Lawrence, Mass. In the last place he remained seven years and then removed to Cambridge, Mass., where he was pastor of the Lee Street Unitarian Society for ten years. At the end of that time, February, 1865, he accepted an earnest invitation from the School Committee of the city of New Bedford to take charge of the schools of that city as Superintendent; and in that position he has remained to the present time.

In November, 1838, he married Elizabeth Davis Locke, daughter of Joseph and Mary Locke, of Boston, by whom he has had five children. Two died in infancy. Of those who lived to maturity, the oldest, Frances Sargent, married Henry S. Mackintosh, of Cambridge; the second, Mary Vincent, married James S. Tryon, of Rumford, R. I.; the third, Elizabeth Ingersoll, married John Tetlow, then of New Bedford, subsequently of Boston. She died in March, 1878.

ISAAC HINCKLEY.

MR. HINCKLEY sends the following brief account of his busy and useful life.

PHILADELPHIA, Dec. 27, 1883.

MY DEAR CLASSMATE:

I was born in Hingham, Mass., October 28, 1815. My parents were Isaac and Hannah (Sturgis) Hinckley. In my seventh year I entered the Derby Academy, Hingham, where I was fitted to enter the class of 1833, with my schoolmates, Baker, Eaton and Gay, but was very properly retained at home on account of my youth. In 1830 I entered without conditions with the class of 1834, but passed the Freshman year at home, joining the class at the beginning of the Sophomore year, September, 1831. I shot ducks, kicked football, kept my shooting skiff and studied a little until December, 1832, when, by advice of Dr. Reynolds, at that time the first oculist in Boston, I "took up my connections" temporarily, as I supposed, but in fact never to resume them, until, to my great surprise, I received my degree in 1865, through the kind exertions of some of my classmates. I had always, however, retained my interest in the class, and since 1859, when we had our first class meeting after graduating, I have never failed to dine with them on commencement day.

From 1832 to 1836 I consulted the leading oculists in this country and in England, spending a portion of the time in London. In 1836, convinced that I must renounce all hope of becoming a civil engineer, as I had earnestly desired, I sought position and work in Illinois, at that time distant from Boston ten days by mail route. There I was agent of the Audubon Land Co., and a farmer without hired men. I served the United States as a post-master, the State as a justice of the peace, and the County as a surveyor and commissioner of school lands.

In 1845, worn out by fever and ague, I left the west and entered the service of the Boston and Providence Railroad Co. Till 1848 I represented that company in Providence, and then became Superintendent of the Providence and Worcester Railroad Co. when first operating their road. In 1850 I left active railroad service and became Superintendent of the Merrimac Manufacturing Co. of Lowell, Mass., which office I held till 1865. During most of that period I was a director of the Boston and Lowell Railroad Co., the Lowell Gas Light Co., and the Lowell Institution for Savings. Early in 1865 I accepted the presidency of the Philadelphia, Wilmington and Baltimore Railroad Co., left vacant by the resignation of my old friend and classmate, Samuel M. Felton, whose health was so seriously impaired as to force him to retire after an eminently successful administration of more than thirteen years.

I am still president of the P., W. and B. R. R. Co., and of several other connecting roads, but for two years past I have been relieved from active work, and have much time at my disposal. I have had my full share of physical troubles, but am still reasonably well and able to travel in pursuit of swans, geese and ducks, from Florida to northern Dakota, as I have done this year.

In 1840 I married Julia Randolph Townsend, born in Illinois of parents who emigrated from New York in 1818. We have had born to us four boys and three girls. Of the boys one died in infancy; another, Wallace, Adjutant of the 44th Massachusetts Vol. Infantry, and of the 2d Massachusetts Vol. Heavy Artillery, died in 1865, at the age of twenty-one, at Fort Macon, N. C., having given the last three years of his life to his country's service. Five remain to us, and my dear companion in weal and wo for forty-three years continues to be the chief blessing of my home.

Very truly,
Your friend and classmate,
Isaac Hinckley.

CHARLES MASON.

AS the conventional circumstance of being born, it seems commonly to be expected, will be an item in any biographical sketch, it may be stated here that that event, it is understood, came to me on the 3d day of June, 1810, at Dublin, N. H. My father and mother were Thaddeus, Jr., and Lydia (Perry) Mason, both of Dublin nativity, whose immediate ancestors removed to that place from Sherborn about the year 1765. My paternal lineage is deduced through Capt. Hugh Mason, who came to this country from England in 1634, and settled in Watertown, Mass.

My early years were passed much as those of other farmers' boys at that time; attending the district school for a term of eight or ten weeks in the summer and about the same in winter; after that in the winter only; the rest of the time at work. I began the study of Latin in the autumn after I was eighteen at a private fall school which chanced to be held in the town that year. The succeeding winter I kept a district school, and studied Latin as I had time. The next spring, 1829, I went to Phillips Exeter Academy, where I continued at that time but one term, and spent the rest of the year at home studying, except that in the winter I kept a public school. In the spring succeeding, 1830, I returned to the Academy at Exeter, where I remained four terms, the last year in the advanced class, until August, 1831.

When at Exeter I was a member, and for a time president, of the Golden Branch, and delivered a Valedictory before the Society at the close of my last term at the Academy. And here I ought to recognize, as I do with deep personal satisfaction, my obligations for the encouragement, counsel and aid afforded me at that stage of my education by the Rev. Levi Washburn Leonard, D.D. (H. C. 1815), the minister of my native town, a man of pure and exalted character, of practical good sense, of sound judgment and wise discrimination, of a kindly and genial spirit, one of the "doers of the word" also, whose life was given to arousing the intellectual faculties, refining the feelings and tastes, keeping pure and unsullied the morals, and quickening the spiritual perceptions of the people; whose special devotion and consecration were to the young, and who did more, doubtless, for the common schools of his adopted state than any other man of the day.

In September, after I left Exeter, I entered the Sophomore class in Dartmouth College, where I continued till towards the end of the college year, when I took up my connections with Dartmouth in order to enter at Cambridge, for which I had been, as far as was practicable, preparing for some weeks previous. Unfortunately for me the course of study at Dartmouth was then well nigh a full year behind that of Harvard; but remaining at home the rest of the summer studying by myself, by diligence, persistence, and hard work generally, I was able to accomplish so much, that upon examination, on the first of September, 1832, I was admitted clear to the Junior class of Harvard College.

In those times, some of us found it necessary and were permitted to be absent for a term in the winter to keep school. In the Junior year I had a public school in the centre of Northborough; in the Senior year in the centre of Sterling. With these exceptions I spent the whole of these two years in steady attendance upon the work of the class. The years passed pleasantly, and considering my limited time and opportunities for fitting, and the breaks in my four years' course of study, as profitably and successfully as could reasonably have been anticipated. I graduated in regular course in 1834, and three years later took the degree of A.M.

While in college I was a member of the Hasty Pudding Club and of the Phi Beta Kappa Society. In the latter part of the Junior year I wrote a dissertation which was offered for a Bowdoin prize, and to which the first prize was awarded.

I had intended to spend some time after graduating in teaching; but no eligible place offering at the time, I remained at home through the autumn, and in default of anything specific to do, took up the study of Hebrew by myself; and the next term I spent in the Divinity School at Cambridge. But, at the close of the term, having an opportunity to take the Medford High School, then just opened, I gladly availed myself of it, and had the charge of that institution from May to August. In the course of the summer a tutorship in the Latin department at Harvard College was offered me, which, with some hesitation, I accepted. I entered upon my duties as tutor at the beginning of the fall term of 1835, and held the position for four years. During two and a half years of this time I was also a student in the Dane Law School, and having completed the prescribed course of study, in 1839 I received the degree of LL.B.

After leaving the law school, I spent several months in the office of Messrs. Hubbard and Watts, in Boston, and in September, 1839, was admitted in Boston to practise in the courts of the Commonwealth and in the United States Circuit and District Courts. In June, 1841, I opened an office in Lancaster, where I remained till September, 1842, when I removed to the neighboring town (now the city) of Fitchburg, where I have since resided. In June, 1842, I was appointed one of the standing commissioners in bankruptcy for the Massachusetts District under the United States bankrupt law, and held the office till the law was repealed. Afterwards, I was a Master in Chancery for the County of Worcester, an office which, at that time, had jurisdiction of insolvency proceedings; and in 1851, upon a change in the statutes upon the subject, I was appointed a Commissioner of Insolvency for Worcester County, which office I held till 1853, when I was removed for being a *Free Soiler*, which, undeniably, I was.

I have had but little participation in political or public affairs. I was a member of the House of Representatives of Massachusetts in 1849 and in 1851. In the latter year my position, had I done nothing else, gave me an opportunity to do what I doubt not I shall ever contemplate with profound satisfaction,—to cast the vote, which, in the same sense as did that of every other of the one hundred and ninety-three members who voted for him, after a struggle of more than three months, on the twenty-sixth ballot, elected Charles Sumner to the United States Senate. I was also a member of the Constitutional Convention in 1853.

I was married Aug. 9, 1853, to Caroline Atherton Briggs, youngest daughter of Dr. Calvin and Rebecca (Monroe) Briggs. Dr. Briggs was a graduate of Williams College, 1803, and received the degrees of A.M. and M.B. from Harvard in 1807, and of M.D. in 1811, and was a practising physician in Marblehead for forty-five years. We have one child, Atherton Perry Mason, born Sept. 13, 1856, who graduated at Harvard College in 1879, and in 1882, after completing the regular course of study in the Harvard Medical School, took the degree of M.D., and is settled in the practice of his profession at Fitchburg.

All this, I am aware, only touches some of the *apices—the tips*—without coming very near to the actual grain, the essence and substance of the life. But then the interior phase of an uneventful life, if shown, is of little interest or concern to others.

It has become rather fashionable to decry academical education as of little worth, if not indeed positively harmful to success in life. For myself, I know not for what consideration I would voluntarily part with the memory of my relations, humble as they were, with Phillips Exeter Academy and Harvard College, and the resultant advantages of those relations. It is undeniable, that many a college graduate wofully fails to achieve a life which in any worthy sense can be called successful. But could an accurate account be taken of the number of actual failures in life of college graduates as compared with the whole class of graduates, and of the number of like failures of those not graduates as compared with the whole of that class, I imagine that the percentage of failures in the former class would be found to be surprisingly less than in the latter. Moreover, I confess to a sympathy with a view, which is well expressed by a writer in the *Century* for October, 1883, p. 950. "The main purpose of education is not to promote success in life, but to raise the standard of life itself." I understand the word "success" in this connection in the sense in which I am constrained to believe it lies in the minds of the majority of people, as that success the unit of which, distinctively and always, is *the dollar*. With the idea of attaining to this success, young men instead of laboring thoughtfully and patiently to develop and compact a broad and substantial foundation, suitable, when needed, to receive any desired superstructure, are spurred on to the exclusive culture of one or a few specific faculties, thereby marring the integrity, the wholeness, the symmetrical completeness of their constitution, and rendering themselves in a degree deformed and monstrous; and this to the end that they may the earlier become more effective *machines* for doing work, the whole ultimating practically and mainly as the final cause in their earning more money or perchance acquiring more fame;—both which are, after all, but selfish considerations.

I hold that a man, as one of his race, owes something to himself personally, and not all to his estate or to the world. There is a *success* in which I fully believe, and that is the success whose criterion is not primarily wealth or distinction, but *character*.

CHARLES BRECK PARKMAN.

CHARLES BRECK PARKMAN, son of Charles (H. C. 1803) and Joanna Phillips (Fay) Parkman, was born at Westborough, Mass., June 13, 1813. His preparation for college was made at Leicester Academy.

Though at present in poor health, Mr. Parkman has written briefly as follows in regard to his life.

"My father died soon after my graduation, and I succeeded to his business and attended to the care of his family for several years, until the younger members had grown up, I being the eldest but one of eight, six girls and two boys. For a short time I taught school in Westborough. I also studied medicine one week, until, while studying a medical work one day, I found a confession by the Medical Faculty of Paris, that the practice of medicine was an experiment, and as likely to kill as cure; that, in fact, it was thought more men were killed by it than cured. I afterwards became engaged in trade for two years at St. Louis; then a resident of Madison, Ind., for six years, as clerk in a foundry and railroad office. Thence, in 1849, I went to California, where I remained two years, long enough to find gold sufficient to pay my expenses back. I afterwards resided in this place, Indianapolis, as secretary of a rail-mill, until a few years since. Of course, subject to so many changes in life, I have never married, my father's children (some of them) having been a charge and care to me during much of my and their lives."

JOHN WITT RANDALL.

JOHN WITT RANDALL, son of Dr. John (H. C. 1802) and Elizabeth (Wells) Randall, granddaughter of Samuel

Adams, the great patriot of the Revolution, was born in Boston, Mass., Nov. 6, 1813.

He received his preparatory education at the Boston Latin School, in company with many who were afterwards his classmates in college, by whom his peculiar and marked originality of character is well remembered. Though among them he was not wholly of them, but seemed to have thoughts, pursuits and aspirations to which they were strangers.

This was also the case after he entered college, where his tastes developed in a scientific direction, Entomology being the branch to which he specially devoted himself, though heartily in sympathy with nature in her various aspects. The college did little at that time to encourage or aid such pursuits; but Mr. Randall pursued the quiet tenor of his way till he had a very fine collection of insects and extensive and thorough knowledge on that and kindred subjects, while his taste for poetry and the *belles-lettres* was also highly cultivated.

He studied medicine after graduation, but his acquisitions as a naturalist were so well-known and recognized that he received the honorable appointment of Professor of Zoölogy in the department of invertebrate animals in the South Sea Exploring Expedition (called Wilkes's), which the United States were fitting out about this time.

We can all remember the wearisome delays and jealousies which occurred before the sailing of the Expedition, which finally caused Mr. Randall to throw up his appointment. Since that time he has led a quiet and retired life, devoting himself to his favorite pursuits, adding to them also the collection of engravings, of which he has one of the most rare and original collections in this country. He has also devoted much time to the cultivation and improvement of an ancestral country seat at Stow, Mass., for the ancient trees of which he has an almost individual friendship.

An account of his life and experiences from Mr. Randall's own pen would have been very interesting as well as amusing and witty; for in these qualities he excels. In excusing himself from giving this, he writes as follows:

"As for myself, my life having been wholly private, presents little that I care to communicate to others, or that others would care to know. I cannot even say for myself as much as was contained in Professor Teufelsdröck's epitaph on a famous huntsman, viz. that in a long life he killed no less than ten thousand foxes.

"It might have been interesting in former days to have related adventures of my foot journeys as a naturalist, amid scenes and objects then little known or wholly unknown, where the solitary backwoodsman and his family, sole occupants of a tract of boundless forest, were often so hospitable as to surrender their only bed to the stranger, and huddle themselves together on the floor. But since Audubon published his travels, and railroads have penetrated everywhere, such accounts cease to be original, and indeed the people themselves have become almost everywhere homogeneous. Itineraries fill all the magazines, and natural curiosities little known forty years ago have become long since familiar to the public.

"As for my present self, I will say no more than that for health's sake to be much out-of-doors, I have been for a long time engaged in hydraulic, planting, building, and other improvements on my grounds, which create, it is true, pleasant occupation, but which when compared with wild nature so varied about me, I am impressed with the conviction how inferior are our artificial pleasures to those simple enjoyments of wood, water, air and sunshine, which we have unconsciously and inexpensively in common with the innumerable creatures, equally capable of enjoying them.

"As to my literary works,—if I except scientific papers on subjects long ago abandoned, as one on Crustacea in the Transactions of the Academy of Natural Sciences of Philadelphia; two on Insects in the Transactions of the Boston Society of Natural History; one manuscript volume on the Animals and Plants of Maine, furnished to Dr. Charles T. Jackson to accompany his Geological Survey of that State, and lost by him; Critical Notes on Etchers and Engravers, one volume; classification of ditto, one volume, both in manuscript incomplete and not likely to be completed, together with essays and reviews in manuscript not likely to be published,—my doings reduce themselves to six volumes of poetic works, the first of which was issued in 1856 and reviewed shortly after in the North American, while the others, nearly or partially completed at the outbreak of the civil war, still lie unfinished among the many wrecks of Time, painful to most of us to look back upon, or reflect themselves on a Future whose skies are as yet obscure."

Dr. Randall was never married, and resides with his sister in Roxbury.

SAMUEL WILLIAM RODMAN.

I PROMISED, I believe, at our last class meeting, to write a short sketch of my life. In looking back upon the past I find so little in it of general interest, that I feel sure my friends will agree with my own conclusion, that, the briefer the sketch, the better it will be.

My father, William R. Rodman, was born in New Bedford, Mass. (the family having originally come to Newport, R. I., in 1676), and was sent for some years to Reading, England, for his education. Soon after coming of age he removed to Philadelphia, Pa., and married my mother, Rebecca Waln Morgan, of that city. I was born in Philadelphia, Oct. 30, 1814. The family removed to New Bedford in the autumn of 1829. I was first sent to a school near Philadelphia, then recently opened by a Frenchman named Phiquepal. In 1826 my father took me to Northampton, Mass., and placed me in that famous "Round Hill" boarding school, which had been established not long before by Messrs. Cogswell & Bancroft, and which attracted for years large numbers of boys of the most prominent families in the country, from Maine to Louisiana, from Canada and the

West Indies. At this school I spent nearly four and a half years satisfactorily and pleasantly, leaving it only when I went up to Cambridge for my examination in 1830. The school was conducted on broad and liberal principles. There was a very strong corps of teachers, including Messrs. Felton, Beck, Walker and Hillard, who instructed us in all the usual languages and common branches of education, as well as in drawing, music, singing, dancing, riding, etc. etc. Even at this late day, though so many have passed away, I am constantly meeting in all parts of the world some old "Round Hill" friend and schoolmate.

Of my college life little need be said. I lived the first year at Prof. Farrar's; the two next at Dr. Ware Senior's, and the last in Stoughton Hall. Study never attracted me strongly. I always preferred to wander, gun in hand, on ornithological excursions, with my good friend Prof. Nuttall, who was then publishing his very useful and popular ornithology. After graduating I read law with Judge Warren (H. C. 1817) of New Bedford, and in the spring of 1836 sailed for Europe, where I remained for nearly two years, travelling over the whole continent, and passing some weeks at Algiers in the early days of the French domination. Returning home I went into the whaling business, in which I continued for ten years.

In October, 1838, I was married at King's Chapel, Boston, to Emma, daughter of Thomas Motley, and we have now lived together for more than forty-five years. We have had four children : two sons, both of whom are dead; and two daughters, of whom the eldest was married, and is left a widow with four children.

In 1850 I removed to Boston, and have since resided there and in the neighborhood, with the exception of some ten years spent in Europe, during four journeys, the last not yet completed.

My tastes have always leaned towards an out-of-door life. I have devoted much time to shooting, fishing, riding, and driving; and to this taste added to the inheritance of a good constitution I ascribe the excellent health which I have always enjoyed, and which enables me yet, in my seventieth year, to participate in these, my favorite pursuits, with the same ardor as I could twenty years ago.

JOSEPH SARGENT.

DR. SARGENT sends the following statement in regard to himself.

I was born in Leicester, Mass., Dec. 15, 1815, being the second son of Henry and Elizabeth (Denny) Sargent.

Having received my preparation at Leicester Academy, I entered college in 1830. Graduating with the class in 1834, I entered immediately upon the study of medicine in the office of Dr. Edward Flint, the principal physician in my native town. I remained with him one year, reading a great deal and learning very little. In the autumn of 1835 I went to Boston, and entered the Medical School, being also under private instruction from Dr. James Jackson, Dr. John Ware, Dr. Winslow Lewis, and Dr. George Otis, all Harvard graduates. I retained membership in this school till my graduation in 1837, although I spent about six months in the autumn and winter of 1836 and 1837 in Philadelphia, under instruction from both schools there at that time, the Pennsylvania University and the Jefferson Medical College. These schools were then at constant war with each other, like the Guelphs and Ghibbelines, and it was a wonder to the foolish that I could belong to both. My chum in Philadelphia was our classmate, S. Conant Foster, who afterwards practised medicine in New York.

Returning to Boston in the spring of 1837, I took my medical degree in the August following, and was immediately appointed house physician at the Massachusetts General Hospital, which office I filled for the customary period of one year. In

September, 1838, in company with Dr. William Mack (H. C. 1833), who had been my associate at the Hospital as house surgeon, I sailed for Europe. In Paris mostly and in London for a few weeks I pursued my medical studies till May, 1840, when I sailed for New York. Arriving in the last of May, I opened an office in Worcester, Mass., June 1, 1840. Here I have remained since, working faithfully, with two recesses of nearly one year each spent in Europe for medical improvement, the first in 1850 and the second in 1867 and '68.

Sept. 27, 1841, I married Emily Whitney of Cambridge, sister of the wife of our admirable professor and president Felton, who was nearer to our class because the brother of our excellent and distinguished classmate, Samuel M. Felton. We have had six living children, of whom four survive, two sons and two daughters. The sons are both graduates of Harvard College, Joseph Sargent, Jr., and Henry Sargent, of the classes of 1870 and 1876, and are both married. The daughters remain unmarried.

The foregoing is all of my history that could possibly interest any public, and it was my purpose to stop here; but the suggestion from our historiographer, that these memoirs are not for the public but for the class, prompts me to say more.

The freedom and fulness and confidence with his classmates which may be becoming to the Harvard graduate of fifty years ago, do not, alas! befit the graduate in the large classes of to-day, and would scarcely be appreciated. This ancient and honorable class-interest was an important part of the interest of the graduate in the college itself, threw a halo around its learning and all its happy influences, and contributed largely to its prosperity and success. But this is of the past. The college is now "cosmopolitan," and is "run," to use the language of the day, in a business way, and young men go through its courses as a business operation. They select their own studies, instead of submitting themselves to the guidance and instruction of men wise by learning and experience. The once scholastic campaign is a sort of guerilla operation, irregular, unsteady, discursive, and erratic. When a whole class moved in the same ranks, through the same field, sustaining each other towards the same end, under wise and experienced direction, there was sympathy, fellowship and strength. The field, the fellows, and the end were never forgotten. I write this because I feel it, and it may explain and excuse a more detailed autobiography.

In looking back over the fifty years since our graduation, I take satisfaction in saying, that while I studied medicine as an undergraduate, I studied most assiduously, always far into the night. My thesis for graduation was upon Cicatrization of Tubercular Cavities in the Lungs, and was, so far as I know, the first monograph ever written on this important subject. I read it recently, after it had remained untouched nearly fifty years, and was proud to find it was still good reading. I say this in the consciousness of self-glorification, which is a proper part of one's autobiography to his own classmates of fifty years ago. This essay attracted the attention of Dr. Jacob Bigelow, whose son, the great surgeon, Henry J. Bigelow, was my successor at the Hospital, and who afterwards in his own recovery from gravest disease illustrated the theory of the essay. To the favor of Dr. Jacob Bigelow I have been greatly indebted for what success I have had in professional life.

While in Paris, in 1838 and 1839, I wrote a successful prize essay on Medulla Sarcoma. This essay is far behind the surgery of to-day; but it gave me some distinction at the time, and this was largely increased by its associating me with Dr. Gerhard of Philadelphia, who got the medical prize in the same year of 1840.

My professional life in Worcester has had a certain provincial success; and I have often felt that I got more credit than I deserved. I have endeavored to do good, and to hold high the standard of the medical profession.

Politically, as parties were in 1840, I was a Democrat, and I held to that party so long as it seemed to me to have any fixed principles. Free trade, a sound currency and equal rights designated my political creed. But I was also an abolitionist of the Garrisonian type, my first inspiration coming from Henry

Ware, Jr., Dr. Follen, and the Grimkés in 1832. From my first settlement in Worcester, I was known as an abolitionist, when, to be such, was to be pointed at and stigmatized. Many are the times that I have met as with a few in an upper chamber. Perhaps I am the only one of the class who ever had to do with John Brown, whose spirit afterwards went marching on. I was of a party in 1857 or 1858, with three or four others, where John Brown and Frederic Douglass were the guests at a little supper. No exploits, nor rashness, nor raids were spoken of, but universal humanity alone.

But I have written enough. As boy, as man, as physician, as philanthropist, I believe I have always been consistent. To the class of 1834 I have always been true. And thus I have written the history of my own life, which no other man would ever think worth writing.

ROYALL TYLER.

JUDGE TYLER has sent memoranda for the following brief statement.—T. C.

Royall Tyler, son of Chief Justice Royall (H. C. 1776) and Mary (Palmer) Tyler, was born at Brattleboro', Vermont, April 19, 1812. His name was originally Charles, but was changed to Royall for family reasons by act of Legislature.

He was prepared for college at Phillips Exeter Academy, and entered as Sophomore in 1831. He had a scholarly habit of mind and pleasant wit, which made him a genial and popular companion. He was chosen class poet; but his poem touching more upon the troubles of the times than met the approbation of the Faculty, it was not delivered in the college chapel, but at a class entertainment at Porter's on the evening of Class Day, as will be remembered by all. Like many others he did not take his degree at Commencement in 1834, but received it subsequently in 1847. On leaving college he immediately began the study of law in the office of Charles G. Loring. Esq., of Boston, and was admitted as Attorney and Counsellor of the Supreme Court in 1838, and established himself in his native town of Brattleboro' in 1839, and began the practice of law. He was elected Judge of Probate for the district of Marlboro', which consists of the southern part of the Windham County, in 1846, and has held the office by successive elections up to the present time. He was appointed clerk of all the courts of Windham County in the spring of 1851, and holds the office still.

Mr. Tyler was married to Miss Laura B. Keyes, daughter of Judge Asa Keyes, of Brattleboro', in the spring of 1841. He has had three daughters, one of whom died in infancy, and the other two are married.

CHARLES ELIOT WARE.

CHARLES ELIOT WARE, son of Dr. Henry (H. C. 1785) and Elizabeth (Bowes) Ware, was born in Cambridge, Mass., May 7, 1814.

With the exception of one year passed at the Academy at Lancaster, Mass., he received his education preliminary to entering college at private schools in Cambridge. He entered Harvard in 1830, and graduated in 1834. He immediately entered the Medical School in Boston, and took his medical degree in 1837.

Excepting two visits to Europe, at intervals of twenty years, he has lived and practised his profession in Boston. He was married in 1854, and has one daughter.

CHARLES NEWELL WARREN.

CHARLES NEWELL WARREN, son of Jonas and Dolly (Tucker) Warren, was born in Stow, Mass., July 21, 1818. He received his preparation for college at the Academy in Stow, entering in 1830 at the age of twelve years, and joining the class at the beginning of the last term of the Freshman year in the summer of 1831. He was the youngest member of the class, and was familiarly known as "Little Warren," his size and appearance corresponding to his years. Though so young he was always found adequate to the duties of his position, and graduated creditably in 1834.

After graduating he taught successively at Framingham, Mass., and at Baltimore and Port Deposit, Md. In the winter of 1836 he went to Kentucky with the intention of practising civil engineering; but being made professor of mathematics in Bacon College, Georgetown, Ky., he remained there one year. He then entered upon the practice of civil engineering, and continued it for fourteen years. He was engaged first on the Cincinnati and Charleston railroad; then on the road from Frankfort to Lexington; and finally built the railroad from Frankfort to Louisville.

In the year 1843 he married Miss Myra Aldridge, of Lancaster, Ky., and has had a family of seven children, four girls and three boys, all of whom are living.

In 1852 he commenced business as a private banker, and in 1865 became president of a National Bank, in which position he remained for more than thirty years. The institution is thus spoken of in a book called "The Industries of Louisville": "Among the great fiduciary institutions of Louisville 'The Louisville City National Bank' stands prominent, not only for the greatness of its financial weight and the extent of its operations, but, also, on account of the high standing and spotless character of its management. The banking business was established in this city in 1851 by C. N. Warren and J. P. Curtis as a private banking concern, under the name and style of C. N. Warren & Co. During the early years of its existence, the bank was devoted to a general banking and brokerage business, and in that field its manager, Mr. Warren, displayed such shrewd skill and energy as a manipulator of large sums of money, and pursued such an honorable and liberal policy, that his house soon took rank among the most reliable and substantial establishments of the kind in the city, and its proprietor stood among the soundest and ablest of our financialists. In 1865 the bank was reorganized as a National Bank, under the National Banking Act, taking then its present name, with Mr. C. N. Warren as president. The conservative basis upon which it was originally organized has never been impaired, and the principles which were laid down for its guidance thirty years ago by its most prominent founder and present president have been adhered to through every change."

Since the publication of the above Mr. Warren has started a new bank in Louisville,—the Fourth National Bank, a government deposit bank, of which he is president.

No one has shown a greater interest in his Alma Mater and the class of 1834 than Mr. Warren. He has almost invariably been present at commencements and class festivals, and has been a liberal contributor to everything calculated to promote class interests and pleasures.

NOTE.—Mr. Warren being unable to write at present, from impaired vision, the above notice has been prepared by T. C.

HIRAM WELLINGTON.

HIRAM WELLINGTON, son of David and Rebecca (Stearns) Wellington, was born March 14, 1806, in Lexington, Mass., being the oldest member of the class. He lived with his father till about twenty years of age, with no advantages of education except those afforded by the common schools during the winter. Neither his taste nor opportunity for study was likely to be much developed or gratified while under the influences of home, nor were the common schools as then organized able to give him such an education as he desired. The question was, how should he gratify his desire for a better education? He could look to his father for very little encouragement or assistance. He must assume and carry the burden alone if at all. The loss of his mother when he was about fifteen years of age rendered his situation still more discouraging for the attainment of his desire. He was not brilliant, hardly up to mediocrity. Why then did he desire an education? For many reasons, but principally for its intrinsic worth, and because the possession of it would be a constant source of enjoyment of which no one could deprive him. Accordingly he undertook it, and has never repented it.

After leaving college he spent two years in the State of Maine; one year in Castine teaching a private school, and one year in Ellsworth in the law office of Joshua W. Hathaway, Esq. Returning to Cambridge he entered the Harvard Law School, where he completed his studies in 1838. In the summer of that year he was admitted to the Suffolk bar, and took an office in Boston, where he has since resided and practised his profession. He has always enjoyed uninterrupted good health, and has never had occasion to use glasses to enable him to read printing or manuscript.

In October, 1851, he was married to Miss Anne A. Hudson, then of Boston, but a native of Westborough, Mass., with whom he has lived very happily. He is without children.

In their religious associations Mr. Wellington and his wife joined the Park Street Congregational Church, during the pastorate of Rev. Andrew L. Stone, and are still members of that church. He has never sought nor filled any public office, with the exception of a few years' service on the Primary School Committee.

NATHANIEL WEST.

NATHANIEL WEST, son of Nathaniel and Mary Bowles (White) West, was born in Salem, Mass., Oct. 22, 1814.
He received his preparation for college at the Salem Latin School, entered the Freshman class in 1830, passed smoothly through the whole four years, and graduated in 1834. Mr. West was very much interested in all out-of-door exercises, in which he was a proficient; at the present day he would have been the champion of his class in every thing of the sort, having a large and noble person and great physical strength, combined with a most generous and amiable disposition.

Having a taste for field sports and skill in woodcraft, Mr. West knew the haunts and habits of beast, bird or fish for miles around. Cambridge was then comparatively a wild region within a moderate walk of the college, and the discharge of a gun would cause no alarm or disturbance. Thus rural excursions, including shooting or fishing as a side issue, were in vogue for pleasant Saturdays, then largely leisure time, and there was no more skilful leader and guide than he on such occasions. The writer of this notice can well remember a golden holiday passed under his guidance, when, though not himself a sportsman, he was admitted to the mysteries of the gentle art, helping to force a light skiff through the net work of shallow streams, overarched by green boughs, through which the flickering sunlight fell upon the water, which connected Fresh Pond with adjoining waters, and seeing the beautiful wood-duck fall to his unerring gun, or the pickerel flash out of its native element. Ah! those were golden days indeed, to be lived again in memory, but never to return.

Mr. West moved to the West with his father and family, and settled in Indianapolis. For about ten years he was engaged in the farming and milling business, and subsequently in real estate, in which he continued in that city until 1860, when he went to Newton County, settling in Kentland, and still continuing in the real estate business until 1868, when he was elected clerk of the court of Newton County, which office he held nearly three years. Mr. West owned a farm of two hundred and forty acres southwest of Kentland, and desiring to improve it he moved from Kentland, and has continued to reside on the farm. He is well located, with evidence of thrift and good management. He takes an interest in his old associates, but can hardly look forward to attending our meetings, as he has been a victim of muscular rheumatism for many years.

NOTE.—Being unable to use a pen, Mr. West has entrusted me with the preparation of the above notice.—T. C.

JOSEPH HARTWELL WILLIAMS.

JOSEPH HARTWELL WILLIAMS, son of Reuel and Sarah Lowell (Cony) Williams, was born in Augusta, Maine, Feb. 15, 1814, a descendant in the sixth generation from Richard Williams, who came to this country from Glamorganshire, Wales, in 1632, and settled soon after in Taunton, Mass. His grandfather, Seth Williams, came from Easton, Mass., to Augusta in 1779, and in 1781 married Zilpha Ingraham, daughter of Jeremiah Ingraham, who had removed to Augusta from Stoughton, Mass., in 1780.

His father, Reuel Williams, was born in Augusta, June 2, 1783, and although his educational advantages did not extend beyond the academy of his native town, he received the honorary degree of A.M. from Harvard College in 1815. His mother, Sarah Lowell Cony, born July 18, 1784, was a daughter of Daniel Cony, of Sharon, Mass., a young physician, who in 1776 married Susanna Curtis, daughter of Rev. Philip Curtis (H. C. 1738), born in Roxbury, Mass., but settled as pastor of a parish in Sharon. Dr. Cony came to Augusta in 1778, where he died in 1842 at the age of ninety years.

Like his father before him Williams has resided in Augusta from his birth. He was named for a notable kinsman, Joseph Hartwell, a farmer of Massachusetts, whose industry and probity were distinguishing characteristics, and they were faithfully impressed upon his young namesake by his parents as a stimulus to the acquisition of a like honorable reputation. At the age of twelve years he was placed in the family and under the instruction of the Rev. Hezekiah Packard, S.T.D. (H. C. 1787), of Wiscasset, Maine, where he remained about two years, being one of the six boys attending that celebrated private school. In the spring of 1829 he entered the Mt. Pleasant Classical Institute at Amherst, Mass., a school of like grade and distinction as the Round-Hill School at Northampton, Mass., and remained until the summer of 1830, when he entered the Freshman class of Harvard College.

From the outset he showed himself a diligent, not to say an ambitious student, and was recognized as among the most meritorious members of his class by election into the Phi Beta Kappa fraternity at the close of his Junior year. The college honor which he most valued, however, was conferred upon him by his classmates when they chose him Class Orator for the farewell ceremonies of the Senior year.

Upon leaving college in 1834 he became a member of the Dane Law School at Cambridge, at that time under the care of Professors Joseph Story and Simon Greenleaf, whose invaluable instructions he enjoyed for the greater part of two years. Upon receiving the customary degree at graduation he returned home to complete his studies in the law office of his father. He was admitted to the bar in the summer of 1837, and immediately succeeded to the law business of his father, who retired from practice upon being elected a Senator of the United States in 1837.

From that period he devoted himself to his profession until July, 1862, when the decease of his father, and the consequent duty then cast upon him of settling a large estate, made it necessary for him to withdraw from a profession well suited to his taste, and from which he had derived all reasonable satisfaction.

In the early part of 1862 he had received at the hands of Gov. Washburn the gratifying compliment of a nomination to a seat upon the bench of the Supreme Judicial Court of Maine; but in view of the advanced age of his father, then close upon his eightieth year, and other claims of family and kindred, he put aside the tempting offer and declined to accept a position which, under different circumstances, would have been esteemed by him the attainment of his highest aim.

In 1839 he had the honor of a place upon the military staff of Gov. Fairfield, which was not without interest and importance; for the exciting scenes of mustering troops and of military drill which grew out of the menacing attitude of the authorities of New Brunswick in asserting their side of the New England Boundary Dispute, occurred during Gov. Fairfield's spirited administration; but not until 1857 was he called to undertake responsible duties in civil affairs. In early manhood he had become imbued with the political doctrines of Thomas Jefferson, and while at the Law School in Cambridge, in November, 1836, he had cast his maiden ballot in company with classmate Fox in favor of the presidential candidate of the Democrats of that day, and he continued in sympathy with the policy and voted for the candidates of that party till 1854. In that year he was a delegate to a State nominating convention, and was made chairman of its committee on resolutions, but felt constrained to differ from his associates, who insisted upon reporting a resolution to approve the administration of President Pierce, who had signed the act of Congress to repeal the Missouri compromise. A resolution for that purpose, however, was reported by the committee and adopted by the convention, and from that time he ceased to act with that political party as long as the institution of slavery remained a subject of national concern.

In 1854 he took an active part in the presidential campaign, and heartily advocated the election of Fremont, but with no thought of any public promotion following his services in that canvass. On returning home, however, just before the election of that year, he found his name had been placed upon the Republican ticket for Senator for Kennebec by a County convention that had met, acted and adjourned without any previous intimation to him that such a purpose was entertained. The result was his election to the State Senate, and it proved a call to a wider sphere of duty than usually falls to the lot of a Senator. When the senate organized in January, 1857, he was made president of that body, and at the end of six weeks it became his constitutional function to occupy the executive chair in place of Gov. Hamlin who then vacated it to accept the office of United States Senator. He has reason to believe that the duties of the executive office were satisfactorily discharged by the incumbent of it during the remainder of that year.

The vantage ground he thus occupied might well have justified an expectation on his part, under ordinary circumstances, of being continued still longer in that position by a popular election; but the inclination of political friends to take steps in that direction was not encouraged by him. As long as he did not accept prohibition as the initial and final word in sociology, he was not likely to attract the indispensable votes of a body of men organized and pledged to support only one who did. At the close of the year 1857, therefore, he returned to the congenial pursuits of his profession.

In 1860, when warlike preparations became necessary for the suppression of the secession of the southern states, he gave his earnest approval to all measures, state and national, to uphold the Union; and in the autumn of 1863, at the desire of his kinsman and neighbor, Gov. Cony, he consented to accept an election as a Representative in the Legislature if offered to him, and he was accordingly chosen a member of that body for the year 1864, and was subsequently reëlected for the years 1865 and 1866. During these years of legislative service he was one of the standing committee on finance, and chairman of it in 1865 and 1866. He was also during three years a member of other important committees. He heartily advocated the policy of establishing a sinking fund to provide for the reimbursement of existing loans and such as might yet become necessary under the pressure of the war, and drafted the bill for that purpose which became a law Jan. 28, 1865. The text of this act is embodied in the present laws of the state concerning that subject. He regarded himself fortunate in being a member of the Legislature of 1865, as it thus became his privilege to voice the will of his constituents in voting to ratify the amendment of the Constitution of the United States, by which the existence of slavery within their jurisdiction was henceforth prohibited.

In 1874 he again became a member of the House of Representatives, this time by the action of those of his fellow citizens who set up an independent ticket. The election took place during his absence and without consent or knowledge on his part, and the subsequent service was reluctantly undertaken. The radical change made that year in the law governing the Hospital for the Insane was exceedingly objectionable in his view of it, and it was the cause of deep chagrin that he was unable to defeat it.

In August, 1877, he accepted a nomination for Governor, which had been tendered him by the State Convention of Democrats held in the city of Portland in that month. With great reluctance he had permitted his name to be used in that convention, for he had no desire for the office and no faith in the assurance of friends that his well-known independent character would, that year, draw to his support from other parties votes enough to effect his election. The disappointment of their hope was no surprise to him, and he continued, in the enjoyment of his private career, far happier than any public life, however successful, could have made him.

Among the private trusts committed to his hands has been the agreeable duty of fostering the interests and promoting the usefulness of the Cony Female Academy, an institution founded in 1815 by his grandfather Cony, and incorporated Feb. 10, 1818, by the Commonwealth of Massachusetts. He became a member of the Board of Trustees in 1851, and has served ever since in that capacity, and also as their secretary and treasurer. A substantial and attractive brick school-building was erected by the trustees in 1880 upon the site of the old Academy, and it is now devoted—by the consent of the trustees and agreeably to existing laws—to the uses of a Free High School for the city of Augusta. So long as it shall stand it will serve, not only as a monument of the generosity and public spirit of its founder, but as a reminder of the service rendered by his trustees to the cause of sound learning which he had so much at heart.

The subject of this sketch was married Sept. 26, 1842, to Apphia Putnam Judd, of Northampton, Mass., daughter of the distinguished antiquary, Sylvester Judd, and sister of the late Rev. Sylvester Judd (Yale College 1836), who was settled over the Unitarian Church in Augusta, in October, 1840, whose useful pastorate of twelve years (until his death in 1853) is still freshly remembered ; and whose published works in the field of professional and general literature attest his brilliant and versatile genius.

The only child of the marriage was Arthur Lowell Williams, born Aug. 3, 1843; died Dec. 15, 1846.

LIST OF STUDENTS,

SOME TIME IN THE CLASS OF 1834, WHO DID NOT GRADUATE WITH IT.

---

*Ezra Abbot.
*William S. Batchelder.
*Levi Bigelow.
*Samuel Bugbee.
*Samuel S. Fairbanks.
*Benjamin L. Gorham.
*Thomas Hughes.
*Francis Henry Jackson.
*William Shaler Johnston.
*Horace Keating.
?Thomas M. Keith.
?N. K. Lombard.
*Charles S. Newell.
*Theodore Parker.
*Alfred L. Peters.
*John T. Pitman.
*George Rivers.
*Charles F. Schroeder.
*Henry C. Wayne.
*John Harvey Wright.

The connection of most of the above-mentioned with the class of 1834 was exceedingly slight and shadowy. Some were in college but a single term, and were never matriculated; others but a year or less. Almost all died young.

The only ones who identified themselves in any way with the class, appeared at its festivals or meetings, or answered letters of invitation or inquiry, were Messrs.

Ezra Abbot,
Francis Henry Jackson,
Henry C. Wayne,
John H. Wright,

of whom notices are given; also an interesting incident in the early life of Theodore Parker, connecting him with the class of 1834.

NOTICES OF STUDENTS,

SOME TIME IN THE CLASS OF 1834, WHO DID NOT GRADUATE WITH IT.

EZRA ABBOT.

EZRA ABBOT, son of Ezra and Hannah (Poor) Abbot, was born at Andover, Mass., Nov. 27, 1808. He commenced his preparation for college at Phillips Academy, Andover, and finished it at Phillips Academy, Exeter, entering the latter institution in 1827. Having entered college in 1830, he remained till the end of the Sophomore year. Being several years older than most of his classmates, and feeling that a life of work was before him, he had not that love of study in the abstract that would make him patiently give the years of manhood to studies having no direct relation to his future pursuits. He was a man prompt to decide and to act upon his decision. Having chosen the medical profession, therefore, he decided to begin the study of it at once, and leaving college in 1832, pursued his studies at Andover and Lowell, and the Harvard Medical School, where he took his degree of M.D. in 1837. It is probable that he devoted some of the time between leaving college and taking his degree, an interval of five years, to some gainful calling, as it does not appear that he went abroad or otherwise lengthened the usual course of study. He immediately began practice, settling soon after at Canton, Mass., where he remained in full and active professional work till his death.

He was a hard-working and popular physician, much and widely respected and beloved. A schoolmate at Exeter, Rev. Dr. Morison, said of him, "He was a born doctor by his make and the bent of his mind—so quick in decision and action." In his accounts and collections he was excessively careless, and consequently, as is the case with many men devoted to the welfare of the community, his pecuniary gains were very inadequate and short of what they should have been.

Dr. Abbot was twice married: first, in 1839, to Harriet, daughter of Frederic W. Lincoln, late Mayor of Boston, Mass., who died July 22, 1844, leaving one son, Ezra Lincoln Abbot, still living. Ten years after, Dr. Abbot married Caroline Howard Lincoln, by whom he had two sons and a daughter.

Dr. Abbot died of paralysis, April 27, 1872.

FRANCIS HENRY JACKSON.

FRANCIS HENRY JACKSON, son of Dr. James (H. C. 1796) and Elizabeth (Cabot) Jackson, was born in Boston, Mass., July 6, 1815.

He received his preparatory education at the schools of William Wells (H. C. 1796) and D. G. Ingraham (H. C. 1809).

He spent the Freshman and Junior years at college, and on leaving began the study of medicine, but discontinued it to accept the management or superintendency of some iron mines in eastern New York, in which his family were largely concerned. These not proving permanently profitable he returned to Boston, and became a real estate agent, and also a planner and builder of houses, in which vocations he had considerable success. He married Miss Sarah Anne Boott, of Boston, and left two children.

Though he did not graduate, Mr. Jackson always took great interest in the affairs of the class, and attended its meetings and festivals. The annual meeting and dinner took place at his house in Boston on the evening of Commencement, 1873, at which time Mr. Jackson seemed likely to outlive most of his guests; but died suddenly shortly after, July 5, 1873.

THEODORE PARKER.

THEODORE PARKER, son of John and Hannah (Stearns) Parker, was born at Lexington, Mass., Aug. 24, 1810. His connection with the class was not of long duration, as his comparatively mature years and remarkable mental powers made the ordinary amount and rate of college work seem to him entirely trivial and snail-like. After trying it for a short time he obtained permission to take charge of a school in Watertown, Mass., and keep up his connection with the class by passing all examinations with it. It is impossible to say how long this arrangement lasted, but he entered the Harvard Divinity School before the class of 1834 graduated, finished his course in Theology there in 1836, and received the degree of A.M. in 1840.

To attempt any adequate account of so distinguished and well-known a man as Theodore Parker, is altogether beyond the scope and limits of a class history. Full and interesting memoirs of him have been published, and the leading facts of his life are well known. As he touched the college orbit in connection with the class of 1834, it has been thought best to mention him.

One characteristic anecdote connecting him with the college is here given, which is certainly authentic, as it was had from his own lips.

In the August of 1830, Theodore, who was then working on his father's farm in Lexington, Mass., haying being over and harvesting not begun, asked if he could have the use of the horse on a certain day. Receiving a favorable answer, he started early in the morning on horseback, rode down to Cambridge, tied his horse to the fence of the college grounds, and presented himself for examination with the other candidates for admission. Having been successful he rode home, and at the evening meal being questioned as to where he had been, he simply announced that he had entered Harvard College, which was the first intimation that his family had received of his intention to make the attempt.

Thus, amid other work, he had accomplished, as a mere by-play, what usually occupies the whole time of young men for several years with every advantage of direction and instruction.

His wonderful memory, great powers of acquisition, and ability with his pen and tongue, would, no doubt, have gained him all the distinction that can be had in collegiate life had he remained to graduate. What he accomplished in his comparatively short life, dying in 1860, at Florence, in Italy, where he had gone in search of health, is well known to all.

HENRY CONSTANTINE WAYNE.

HENRY CONSTANTINE WAYNE, son of Justice James M. Wayne, of the United States Supreme Court, was born in Savannah, Ga., in 1815.

He left college at the end of the Junior year, entered the West Point Military Academy in 1834, became a second lieutenant in the Fourth Artillery in 1838, and was promoted first lieutenant in the First Artillery in 1842. He was assistant instructor in military and cavalry tactics at West Point from 1841 to 1843, and was made captain and quartermaster in 1846. He served with the army in Mexico, and was brevetted Major for gallant and meritorious services at Contreras and Cherubusco.

Soon after the annexation of the territory acquired from Mexico, in the absence of railroads, etc., the question of transportation through that vast region awakened the lively interest of the government, and it is believed that Major Wayne first broached the idea of using camels for that purpose. At all events, he was commissioned to visit Egypt and other oriental countries, with instructions to study the habits and capacities of these "ships of the desert," with the view to their importation into this country. He made a thorough study of the subject, and upon his report the government imported a large number of these beasts into Texas.

At the breaking out of the late war, when Georgia seceded, Major Wayne cast in his fortunes with his native State, and was appointed quartermaster-general of Georgia. It was to his knowledge of the details of military requirements that the troops sent from Georgia to the theatre of war owed the completeness of their equipment. His devotion to the service of the side he had taken, was unsparing, and towards the close of the struggle he received the command of a brigade, and was with the little army that disputed Sherman's march through the State.

When peace returned, Gen. Wayne entered upon the lumber and commission business, but after a number of years retired. He was United States Commissioner for several years, and was instrumental in securing justice for the people of his section.

Gen. Wayne was a fluent and thoughtful writer, and contributed often to the columns of the newspapers. He was also the author of several professional works, among which may be mentioned, "A Manual of Sword Exercise." He was very self-sacrificing in the cause of humanity when the yellow fever swept Savannah, and staid as a nurse when so many others fled in dismay.

Gen. Wayne was twice married, and leaves several children by his first wife.

JOHN HARVEY WRIGHT.

JOHN HARVEY WRIGHT, son of John S. and Mary (Wellman) Wright, was born at Piermont, N. H., May 7, 1815. Coming to Boston in 1825, he was placed in the Public Latin School, and entered Harvard in 1830. His name appears in the catalogue of the Freshman year only, and he graduated at Amherst in 1834.

He received his medical education at the Harvard Medical School, and entered the navy as Assistant Surgeon in 1839. From this date, for a period of twenty years, he was in nearly constant active service, when, his health failing, he was retired in 1861 "for long and continued service," holding at his death the office of "Medical Director" under the act of March 2, 1871.

During Dr. Wright's long period of active service, he visited many quarters of the world,—the East Indies three times, the coast of Africa, the Mediterranean, and Mexico. He was present at the storming of Vera Cruz, the loss of the Somers, and at the bombardment of the Barrier Forts, including five days operations. His letters from China and Mexico, published in Harper's Magazine, interested many readers, and gave proof of the literary ability of the writer.

He had a passion for books and engravings, and had made a collection of both, perhaps unsurpassed by that of any private individual, which was unfortunately destroyed in the great fire. He was a man of great culture and sound judgment, which made him always interesting and instructive; but what endeared him most to all who ever came in contact with him, was his unvarying sweetness of disposition, under the painful disease from which he suffered. No one ever saw him angry or even irritable.

Feb. 5, 1863, Dr. Wright married Miss Anna M. Nichols, daughter of Lyman Nichols, Esq., of Boston, who survives him, with two young sons.

Dr. Wright died Dec. 26, 1879.

Though his connection with Harvard College was brief, and he graduated elsewhere, when he became a resident of Boston he identified himself with his first Alma Mater and the class of 1834, which he had entered, and took a lively interest in all class affairs.

www.ingramcontent.com/pod-product-compliance
Lightning Source LLC
Chambersburg PA
CBHW020122170426
43199CB00009B/598